THE INVISIBLE EMPIRE

A bibliography of the
Ku Klux Klan

WILLIAM H. FISHER

The Scarecrow Press, Inc.
Metuchen, N.J., & London
1980

Library of Congress Cataloging in Publication Data

Fisher, William Harvey, 1950-
  The invisible empire.

  Includes indexes.
  1. Ku-Klux Klan--Bibliography. 2. Ku Klux Klan
(1915-   )--Bibliography. I. Title.
Z1249.K8F54   [E668]   016.3224'2'0973   80-10133
ISBN 0-8108-1288-6

ACKNOWLEDGMENTS

I would like to take this opportunity to thank a number of people whose cooperation and help made the successful completion of this bibliography possible. The special-collections librarians and archivists who provided information concerning KKK manuscript material in their collections; the interlibrary-loan people at a number of libraries across the country, and especially within the state of California, who provided much-needed and often obscure material with great speed; Norma Carlsen of our interlibrary-loan department at CSU-Dominguez Hills, who processed the avalanche of requests I submitted; and my fellow librarians and friends at Dominguez Hills, who have all become authorities on the Ku Klux Klan (and are still talking to me)--all provided invaluable help in the compilation of this bibliography. I thank you all.

TABLE OF CONTENTS

INTRODUCTION

In 1866 six men sitting around a fire in the small town of Pulaski, Tennessee, decided to form an organization. The purpose of the group was to frighten the newly freed Negro citizens of the area into remaining under the influence and domination of their old masters. The men felt they could appeal to the superstitious nature of the Negro by wearing outlandish costumes and engaging in wild pranks to lend a supernatural air to their activities. To ensure the success of their activities and to avoid being arrested by the authorities, the men wore masks and kept their identity a secret. The group named itself the Ku Klux Klan, and from its childish beginnings 114 years ago, the KKK has made a unique place for itself in the history of this country. What is unique about the Klan is not that it is a prime example of the intolerance and bigotry that can exist in a society--unfortunately there are more examples of that in our history than one might care to think about. The Klan is unique in the respect that this group is now into its second century of existence; it has gone through at least three distinct phases in that time, and after having virtually "died" at the end of the first two phases it was brought "back to life" and allowed to continue its program of hate and prejudice. This means that the Klan has appealed to at least some element in American society for over 100 years, and, despite repeated attempts to remove the Klan from the scene, it has been able to reappear and re-establish itself within the social fabric in some fashion. Any group that can accomplish such a feat finds that it is strongly supported by some and fiercely opposed by others. The Ku Klux Klan is no exception, as the literature in this volume points out; for the small group that started in a quiet town in Tennessee and its successors have generated a great deal of discussion, study, and debate over its principles, activities, and even its right to exist.

This bibliography is an attempt to compile the bulk of the English-language material dealing with the Ku Klux Klan, up to the year 1978. It is divided into two parts, the 19th

and 20th centuries. This will allow users to direct their at-
tention to the time period of greater interest. Citations for
material dealing with the KKK from both periods are listed
in each section; however, the annotation is only found with
the first citation. Annotations have been provided where possible; in cases where the material was not reviewed only the
bibliographic citation appears. Within each section citations
have been further divided by the kind of material. Newspaper articles have been omitted; however, some citations
from "underground newspapers" of the late '60s and early
'70s were included to give some indication of their coverage
of the Klan. The government documents included represent
only the major committee reports that deal with the KKK;
comments and speeches about the Klan by individual members
of Congress have been omitted.

Users should be advised that if they wish to obtain
further information concerning any of the manuscript/archival
collections listed, they should request information about specific items, since the staffs of the libraries where these collections are located are too small to do subject searches.

Users may also wish to look into three additional
sources of information about the KKK. First, the anti-Klan
laws passed by various states (in an effort to make it difficult for the Klan to operate within their borders) and any
subsequent legal action that resulted from this kind of legislation. Second, the magazines and newspapers published by the
Klan itself, such as the Imperial Night Hawk (Atlanta, 1923-
24) and the Kourier (Atlanta, 1924-36), both put out by the
national Ku Klux Klan organization. A good many of these
publications, such as the Watcher on the Tower (Seattle,
1923), were published by local KKK organizations for a short
time only, making it difficult to verify their existence and
even harder to locate a copy. The third source is a series
of articles that appeared in 1921 in the New York World.
The articles were intended to expose the "revived" KKK of
Imperial Wizard William J. Simmons (which was still basically a southern organization) and arouse public opinion. While
it might have accomplished that goal, the World articles also
gave the Klan some national exposure, which helped that
group gain nationwide support and go beyond its traditional
southern boundaries.

The author and subject indexes should allow both the
serious researcher and the casual reader to find material of
interest on the various aspects of the Klan. It is my hope

that any user will learn as much about the Ku Klux Klan from using this bibliography as I did in compiling it.

William Fisher
California State University,
Dominguez Hills
December, 1978

PART I

THE KLAN OF THE 19th CENTURY

SECTION A: DISSERTATIONS, MANUSCRIPTS/ARCHIVES,
GOVERNMENT DOCUMENTS

Dissertations

A1   Bell, William D.   "The Reconstruction Ku Klux Klan:
      A Survey of the Writings on the Klan with a Profile
      and Analysis of the Alabama Klan Episode, 1866-
      1874. "   Unpublished Ph. D. dissertation, Louisiana
      State University and Agricultural & Mechanical Col-
      lege, 1973.

      An analysis of the writings on the Klan and how they
      have challenged traditional views of the KKK and a
      study of the strength and activities of the Klan in
      Alabama.

A2   Bouge, Jesse P. , Jr.   "Violence and Oppression in
      North Carolina During Reconstruction, 1865-1873. "
      Unpublished Ph. D. dissertation, University of Mary-
      land, 1973.

      The KKK is seen as an instrument used to control
      the excesses of the Union League and free Negroes
      in North Carolina.   The violence employed by the
      Klan is also viewed as a result of earlier violent
      acts by Regulator groups during the initial stages of
      Reconstruction.

A3   Kirkland, John R.   "Federal Troops in the South Atlan-
      tic States During Reconstruction: 1865-1877. "   Un-
      published Ph. D. dissertation, University of North
      Carolina, 1968.

      This study of the role of the U. S. Army during Re-
      construction discusses the reluctance of commanders
      to use their troops in support of "radical" govern-
      ments, which encouraged KKK activities, leading

some areas to form Negro militia units, which led to further Klan activity.

A4   Richardson, Joseph M. "The Negro in the Reconstruction of Florida, 1865-1877." Unpublished Ph. D. dissertation, Florida State University, 1963.

A discussion of the conditions in Florida that led to the rise of the KKK and its activities, which continued until Democratic rule had been restored.

A5   Swinney, Everette. "Suppressing the Ku Klux Klan: The Enforcement of the Reconstruction Amendments, 1870-1874." Unpublished Ph. D. dissertation, University of Texas, 1966.

A study of the effectiveness of the three Enforcement Acts (1870-71) in halting the activities of the KKK throughout the South (see C49).

Manuscript/Archival Collections

A6   Adams, Crawford C. Papers. Manuscript Department, Perkins Library, Duke University.

A7   Aglionby, Frances Y. Papers. Manuscript Department, Perkins Library, Duke University.

A8   Akerman, Amos T. Letterbooks. Manuscripts Department, Alderman Library, University of Virginia.

Correspondence about the suppression of the KKK can be found in this collection of material of the U. S. Attorney-General, 1870-71.

A9   American Missionary Association. Archives. Amistad Research Center, Dillard University.

Correspondence from missionary teachers written during Reconstruction describe Klan activities throughout the South.

A10   Ames Family. Papers. Manuscript Department, Perkins Library, Duke University.

A11   Archbell, Lillie V. Papers. Southern Historical Collection, Wilson Library, University of North Carolina.

Material concerning KKK activities in the Lenior, North Carolina, area.

A12 Ball, William W. Papers. Manuscript Department, Perkins Library, Duke University.

A13 Bernard, George S. Papers. Manuscript Department, Perkins Library, Duke University.

A14 Bond, Hugh L. Papers. Library, Maryland Historical Society.

Letters and other papers written by Bond while he was serving as a judge during the KKK trials in North and South Carolina.

A15 Bratton Family. Papers. Manuscripts Division, South Caroliniana Library, University of South Carolina.

This collection contains material concerning John and Rufus Bratton, who left South Carolina after the passage of the Force Act of 1871 rather than risk arrest in connection with KKK activities.

A16 Bryant, John E. Papers. Manuscript Department, Perkins Library, Duke University.

A17 Buchanan, Robert C. Papers. Library, Maryland Historical Society.

The papers and correspondence of a U. S. Army officer who was stationed in Louisiana for two years and had to deal with Klan activity in that state.

A18 Campbell, Lewis E. Papers. Special Collections, Morris Library, Southern Illinois University.

Copies of a report on a confrontation between Klan members and Negroes in Huntsville, Alabama, are contained in this collection.

A19 Civil War and Reconstruction. Papers. Division of Archives and History, North Carolina Department of Cultural Resources.

This collection contains two items of interest: one is a threatening note signed by the KKK, and the other is an affidavit recounting the events of the murder of the Radical state senator John "Chicken" Stevens.

A20   Debaillon, Paul, and Family.   Papers.   Southwestern Archives and Manuscripts Collection, Center for Louisiana Studies, University of Southwestern Louisiana.

Material concerning Ku Klux Klan activities in Lafayette Parish, Louisiana, is contained in this collection.

A21   Dixon, Thomas, Jr.   Papers.   Dover Library, Gardner-Webb College.

This collection contains manuscripts and personal papers of the author of The Clansman and other KKK-related works (see B39-B42).

A22   Dobbins, John S.   Papers.   Special Collections, Robert W. Woodruff Library for Advanced Studies, Emory University.

This collection contains material concerning KKK activities in Georgia.

A23   Dorsey Family.   Papers.   Manuscript Department, Missouri Historical Society.

A description of the ease with which suspected Klan members were arrested and imprisoned in the Louisville, Kentucky, area.

A24   Ellington, L. S.   Papers.   Manuscript Department, Perkins Library, Duke University.

A25   Elliott, Collins D.   Papers.   Manuscripts Section, Tennessee State Library and Archives.

Correspondence and other material concerning KKK activities.

A26   Fleming, Walter L.   Historical Collections.   Manuscripts and Archives Division, New York Public Library.

Material used by the author in researching the Klan for subsequent publications (see B48-B51, C12, C13).

A27   Fox, John.   Papers.   Manuscript Department, Perkins Library, Duke University.

A28   Fraser, Fredrick.   Letters.   Manuscript Department, Perkins Library, Duke University.

A29   Fuller-Thomas Family.   Papers.   Manuscript Department, Perkins Library, Duke University.

A30   Georgia, State of.   Miscellaneous Papers.   Manuscript Department, Perkins Library, Duke University.

A31   Glenn, Andrew W., and Family.   Papers.   Division of Archives and Manuscripts, Minnesota Historical Society.

This collection contains correspondence addressed to Glenn's wife describing conditions in Nashville, Tennessee, including the flogging of a Negro by the Klan.

A32   Gould, John M.   Papers.   Manuscript Department, Perkins Library, Duke University.

A33   Hale, William D., and Family.   Papers.   Division of Archives and Manuscripts, Minnesota Historical Society.

Correspondence and other material sent to Hale describing KKK activities in Arkansas, where Hale had resided for a short time after the Civil War.

A34   Harrington, George R.   Papers.   Manuscript Department.   Missouri Historical Society.

This collection contains material relating to Harrington's work on William Chisholm, a judge in Mississippi, and his opposition to the KKK.

A35   Hayne, Paul H.   Papers.   Manuscript Department, Perkins Library, Duke University.

A36   Hedrick, Benjamin S.   Papers.   Manuscript Department, Perkins Library, Duke University.

A37 Hemphill Family. Papers. Manuscript Department, Perkins Library, Duke University.

A38 Hickman Family. Papers. Western Historical Manuscript Collection/State Historical Society of Missouri Manuscripts, Ellis Library, University of Missouri.

Correspondence of Thaddeus Hickman concerning the activity of the Ku Klux Klan in Louisiana.

A39 Hoke, William A. Papers. Southern Historical Collection, Wilson Library, University of North Carolina.

Correspondence concerning the activities of the North Carolina Klan in the 1870s.

A40 Holden, William W. Papers. Division of Archives and History, North Carolina Department of Cultural Resources.

This collection of Holden papers contains letters from North Carolina residents concerning their harassment by the KKK.

A41 _____. Papers. Manuscript Department, Perkins Library, Duke University.

The papers of the Reconstruction governor of North Carolina contain a great deal of information concerning Klan activities in that state and Holden's attempts to bring them to a halt.

A42 _____. Papers. Southern Historical Collection, Wilson Library, University of North Carolina.

These Holden papers contain correspondence concerning Klan violence in North Carolina.

A43 Howell, Robert P. Memoirs. Southern Historical Collection, Wilson Library, University of North Carolina.

A discussion of KKK activities in the Goldsboro, North Carolina, area is included in Howell's memoirs.

A44   Johnston, John W.   Papers.   Manuscript Department,
      Perkins Library, Duke University.

A45   Jones, Charles E.   Papers.   Manuscript Department,
      Perkins Library, Duke University.

A46   Keitt, Ellison S.   Papers.   Manuscripts Division, South
      Caroliniana Library, University of South Carolina.

      Included in this collection is a file of newspaper
      clippings concerning KKK activities in South Carolina.

A47   Kilgo, John C.   Papers.   Archives, Perkins Library,
      Duke University.

A48   Kinyoun, John H.   Papers.   Manuscript Department,
      Perkins Library, Duke University.

A49   Ku Klux Klan.   Miscellaneous materials.   Department
      of Archives and History, State of Georgia.

      Material concerning the Ku Klux Klan is scattered
      throughout this department's collection; however, no
      index to specific KKK references exists.

A50   _____.   Papers.   Manuscript Department, Missouri
      Historical Society.

      Documents, pamphlets, and other material concern-
      ing the history of the 19th-century Klan.

A51   _____.   Papers.   Manuscript Department, Perkins
      Library, Duke University.

A52   Larwill, William C. , and Sons.   Papers.   Western
      Historical Manuscript Collection/State Historical
      Society of Missouri Manuscripts, Ellis Library, Uni-
      versity of Missouri.

      Material concerning the Klan's presence and activities
      in Ohio is contained in this collection of papers by
      Larwill and his sons Joseph and John.

A53   Lipscomb Family.   Papers.   Southern Historical Col-
      lection, Wilson Library, University of North Caro-
      lina.

Correspondence concerning KKK activities in the area of Spartanburg, South Carolina.

A54 Martin, Sue A. Papers. Manuscript Department, Perkins Library, Duke University.

A55 Matton, William G. Papers. Manuscript Department, Perkins Library, Duke University.

A56 Nash Family. Papers. Southern Historical Collection, Wilson Library, University of North Carolina.

Material concerning KKK activities in North Carolina.

A57 National Archives. Records.

The official records of a number of government bodies that have had dealings with the KKK are contained in the National Archives. Collections of interest include the records of Congressional committees investigating conditions in the South during Reconstruction, army commands in military districts established during Reconstruction, district court proceedings of KKK trials, and Justice Department files on Klan activities in the 20th century.

A58 North Carolina, State of. Miscellaneous papers. Manuscript Department, Perkins Library, Duke University.

A59 Pearson, Richmond M. Papers. Southern Historical Collection, Wilson Library, University of North Carolina.

A discussion of the KKK in North Carolina and the investigation of its activities by the U. S. government is included in this collection.

A60 Potts Family. Papers. Manuscript Department, Perkins Library, Duke University.

A61 Raines, Edgar F. Papers. Special Collections, Morris Library, Southern Illinois University.

The author's paper "The Ku Klux Klan in Illinois, 1867-1875, " is contained in this collection.

A62 Remmel, Harmon L. Papers. Special Collections, Library, University of Arkansas.

This collection of papers of a prominent member of the Republican Party in Arkansas contains references to his opposition to the Ku Klux Klan.

A63 Robins, Marmaduke S. Papers. Southern Historical Collection, Wilson Library, University of North Carolina.

This collection contains correspondence about the Ku Klux Klan Act of 1870.

A64 Russell, Daniel L. Papers. Southern Historical Collection, Wilson Library, University of North Carolina.

Correspondence describing Klan activities in Sampson County, North Carolina.

A65 Scarborough Family. Papers. Manuscript Department, Perkins Library, Duke University.

A66 Schenck, David. Papers. Southern Historical Collection, Wilson Library, University of North Carolina.

Material concerning Schenck's association with the KKK in the vicinity of Lincolnton, North Carolina.

A67 Shotwell, Nathan. Papers. Southern Historical Collection, Wilson Library, University of North Carolina.

This collection contains correspondence from a man imprisoned for his association with the KKK.

A68 Simpson, William D. Papers. Manuscript Department, Perkins Library, Duke University.

A69 Slavery and Abolition Collection. Miscellaneous materials. Schomburg Center for Research in Black Culture, New York Public Library.

Documents, correspondence, speeches, and other material of interest for a study of the Reconstruction Klan can be found in this collection.

A70 Smith, Luther R. Papers. Manuscript Department, Missouri Historical Society.

A description of KKK activities that were made in an effort to get Smith to resign his judgeship in Alabama.

A71   Stephens, Alexander H.   Papers.   Special Collections, Robert W. Woodruff Library for Advanced Studies, Emory University.

Correspondence and other material concerning KKK activities.

A72   Stevens, Walter B.   Scrapbooks.   Western Historical Manuscript Collection/State Historical Society of Missouri Manuscripts, Ellis Library, University of Missouri.

Newspaper clippings of reports of Klan activity in Missouri.

A73   Swann-Cavett Family.   Papers.   Mitchell Memorial Library, Mississippi State University.

This collection contains correspondence and other material about a former Grand Cyclops of the Mississippi Klan.

A74   Tennessee Historical Society.   Miscellaneous collection. Manuscripts Section, Tennessee State Library and Archives.

This collection contains copies of two KKK constitutions.

A75   Thomas, Ella G.   Journals.   Manuscript Department, Perkins Library, Duke University.

A76   Warmouth, Henry C.   Papers.   Southern Historical Collection, Wilson Library, University of North Carolina.

This collection contains a warning from the Klan dated April 27, 1868.

Government Documents

A77   Proceedings in the Ku Klux Trials at Columbia, S. C.,

in the United States Circuit Court (4th Circuit), November Term, 1871. Columbia, S. C.: Republican Printing Company, 1872.

This volume contains the transcript of the proceedings against members of the KKK in South Carolina. The testimony given by government witnesses provides examples of the activities carried out by the Klan. These trials were one of the major efforts taken against the Klan by the federal government during Reconstruction.

A78 Report of the Joint Select Committee to Inquire into the Condition of Affairs in the Late Insurrectionary States. 13 vols. Washington, D. C.: Government Printing Office, 1872.

The full text of the Select Committee's report, with the testimony of witnesses ranging from Negro victims of the KKK to Gen. Nathan Forrest, the Klan's Grand Wizard, is contained in these 13 volumes, making them one of the most complete chronicles of the Ku Klux Klan available for the Reconstruction era.

B1 An Adventure with the Ku Klux Klan. Hull, Que. :
    Burtt Brothers, 1916.

    A northern Quaker recounts a confrontation he had
    with the KKK while working on the railroad in the South.

B2 Alexander, Thomas B. Political Reconstruction in Ten-
    nessee. Nashville, Tenn. : Vanderbilt University
    Press, 1950.

    An account of the organization of the Klan in Ten-
    nessee (where the Klan was first organized), the ac-
    tivities of the order, and the efforts on the part of
    Radical governor William G. Brownlow to put an end
    to the KKK.

B3 Allen, James S. Reconstruction; The Battle for Democ-
    racy (1865-1876). New York: International Publish-
    ers, 1937.

    An account of KKK attempts to restore Democratic
    leadership in the South through coercive and violent
    means, while Negro militia units tried to hold the
    Klan in check.

B4 Alligood, Katherine (Porter). The Flaming Cross; A
    Novel of the Klan in Alabama in the 1880's. New
    York: Exposition Press, 1956.

B5 Alvarez, Joseph A. From Reconstruction to Revolu-
    tion: The Blacks' Struggle for Equality. New York:
    Atheneum, 1971.

    Examples of Klan activity during Reconstruction, its
    "revival" in the 1920s, and the recent civil-rights
    struggle.

B6   Aptheker, Herbert, ed. A Documentary History of the
      Negro People in the United States. New York: Cita-
      del Press, 1951.

      Reprints of various documents relating to the Klan,
      including testimony about KKK raids and methods by
      some of the victims, and statements of black mem-
      bers of Congress condemning the Klan.

B7   Avary, Myrta L. Dixie After the War; An Exposition
      of Social Conditions Existing in the South, During the
      Twelve Years Succeeding the Fall of Richmond. New
      York: Doubleday, Page & Company, 1906.

      The Klan is seen as one of a number of secret soci-
      eties that developed to combat the rule of Radical
      Republicanism. Examples of KKK activities are in-
      cluded in this rather sympathetic treatment of the
      Klan.

B8   Baughman, Laurence A. Southern Rape Complex;
      Hundred Year Psychosis. Atlanta: Pendulum Books,
      1966.

      The Klan is seen as having been formed to "protect
      the flower of Southern womanhood" and as a reaction
      to the "symbolic rape" of the South by Northerners
      and Freedmen.

B9   Beard, James M. K. K. K. Sketches, Humorous and
      Diadactic, Treating the More Important Events of the
      Ku Klux Klan Movement in the South. With a Dis-
      cussion of the Causes Which Gave Rise to It, and
      the Social and Political Issues Emanating from It.
      Philadelphia: Claxton, Remsen & Haffelfinger, 1877.

      One of a few contemporary attempts to chronicle the
      deeds of the KKK, this volume deals with how the
      Klan got started; its organization; its activities, es-
      pecially in Tennessee; and its eventual decline.

B10   Benedict, Michael L. The Fruits of Victory: Alterna-
      tives in Restoring the Union, 1865-1877. Phila-
      delphia: J. B. Lippincott Company, 1975.

      This work contains reprints of documents concern-
      ing the Klan. Included are excerpts from the testi-

mony given by three Georgia political leaders before the Joint Select Committee to Inquire into the Conditions of Affairs in the Late Insurrectionary States; letters from the papers of Governor William Holden of North Carolina concerning a murder committee by the KKK; and the text of the Ku Klux Klan Act.

B11   Bennett, Lerone, Jr.   Black Power U. S. A. ; The Human Side of Reconstruction, 1867-1877.   Chicago: Johnson Publishing Company, 1967.

The KKK is viewed as a form of "white backlash" to Radical rule in the South. The methods used by the Klan to aid in the restoration of white control are also examined.

B12   Blaustein, Albert P. , and Robert L. Zangrando, eds. Civil Rights and the American Negro: A Documentary History.   New York: Trident Press, 1968.

This volume includes a reprint of the Ku Klux Klan Act (1871) and the legal interpretations and changes resulting from that document.

B13   Bowers, Claude.   The Tragic Era; The Revolution After Lincoln.   New York: Halcyon House, 1929.

This history of Reconstruction includes a discussion of how the KKK got started and subsequent legislation to restrict its activities.

B14   Brawley, Benjamin G.   A Social History of the American Negro.   New York: Macmillan Company, 1921.

Includes a discussion of the "Hamburg Massacre" involving the Klan in South Carolina.

B15   Brewester, James.   Sketches of Southern Mystery, Treason and Murder.   The Secret Political Societies of the South, Their Methods and Manners.   The Phagedenic Cancer on Our National Life.   Milwaukee: Evening Wisconsin Co. , 1903.

A description of the organization of the KKK and examples of Klan activities against Negroes and "carpetbaggers" in various southern states.

B16 Brooks, Ulysses R. , ed. Stories of the Confederacy. Columbia, S. C. : State Company, 1912.

Includes a chapter on the KKK in which it is viewed as providing a means of protection for the ex-Confederate soldier and his family.

B17 Brown, William G. The Lower South in American History. New York: Macmillan Company, 1902.

A discussion of the origins and development of the KKK as it spread from its beginnings in Tennessee throughout the South. The violence used by the Klan against Negroes and whites helping the Freedman is also examined.

B18 Bryant, Benjamin. Experience of a Northern Man Among the Ku-Klux; or the Condition of the South. Hartford, Conn. : The Author, 1872.

B19 Buckmaster, Henrietta. Freedom Bound. New York: Macmillan Company, 1965.

A discussion of Klan activities to prevent Negroes from voting and to encourage support of Democratic candidates in various elections during Reconstruction, and southern reaction to the anti-KKK Enforcement Acts of 1870-71.

B20 Burton, Annie C. The Ku Klux Klan. Los Angeles: Warren T. Potter, Publisher and Bookmaker, 1916.

A copy of the revised Prescript, or constitution, of the KKK is included in this tract aimed at glorifying the Klan as the group that saved the South from the disorder that followed the war.

B21 Carter, Hodding. The Angry Scar; The Story of Reconstruction. Garden City, N. Y. : Doubleday & Company, 1959.

A description of the founding of the Klan and some of its activities is presented, along with a discussion of the anti-Klan measures passed by Congress.

B22 Clark, Thomas D. , and Albert D. Kirwan. The South

Since Appomattox; A Century of Regional Change.
New York: Oxford University Press, 1967.

A discussion of the three "phases" of the KKK, including the organization and activities of the Reconstruction Klan, its activities during the '20s, and its
involvement in the recent civil-rights movement.

B23   Clayton, Powell.   The Aftermath of the Civil War in
      Arkansas.   New York: Neale Publishing Company,
      1915.

      In his own account of the post-war situation, Gover-
      nor Powell Clayton of Arkansas relates how the KKK
      got started in Arkansas, some of the outrages and
      murders committed by the Klan, how Clayton suc-
      cessfully curbed KKK activities, and how the Klan
      had marked him for assassination.

B24   Coleman, Charles H.   Election of Eighteen Sixty Eight;
      The Democratic Effort to Regain Control.   New York:
      Columbia University Press, 1933.

      The Klan's role in the election of 1868 and reactions
      to KKK activities are discussed.

B25   Conway, Alan.   The Reconstruction of Georgia.   Min-
      neapolis: University of Minnesota Press, 1966.

      An analysis of the organization and activities of the
      KKK in Georgia, led by former Confederate General
      John B. Gordon.

B26   Cook, Walter H.   Secret Political Societies in the South
      During the Period of Reconstruction.   Cleveland:
      Press of the Evangelical Publishing House, 1914.

      A discussion of the organization and activities of the
      KKK as the largest and best known of the secret
      societies of the era.   The Klan is credited with
      securing home rule for the southern states and keep-
      ing the newly freed Negroes at their jobs.

B27   Coulter, E. Merton.   The South During Reconstruction.
      Vol VIII of A History of the South.   Edited by
      Wendell H. Stephenson and E. Merton Coulter.   10
      vols.   Baton Rouge: Louisiana State University
      Press, 1947.

A discussion of the post-war Klan, including reasons for its formation, its organization, structure, and activities, and anti-Klan measures.

B28   Cox, Samuel S.   Three Decades of Federal Legislation, 1855 to 1885.   Providence, R. L: J. A. & R. A. Reid, Publishers, 1894.

A description of the KKK influence in the southern states during Reconstruction. Examples of Klan activities and various anti-Klan measures are also provided.

B29   Current, Richard N. , ed.   Reconstruction, 1865-1877. Englewood Cliffs, N. J. :   Prentice-Hall, Inc. , 1965.

This volume contains reprints of three excerpts from the Report of the Joint Select Committee to Inquire into the Conditions of Affairs in the Late Insurrectionary States, including an interview with Nathan Bedford Forrest, testimony of a Negro attacked by the Klan, and testimony of a Klan leader from Georgia. Also included is an excerpt from Senator John Sherman's speech in support of anti-Klan legislation.

B30   Curry, Richard O. , ed.   Radicalism, Racism, and Party Realignment; The Border States During Reconstruction.   Baltimore: Johns Hopkins Press, 1969.

A description of the activities of the KKK in the "border states, " particularly Kentucky and Tennessee, and the effects of the Klan's presence on the political "reconstruction" of these states.

B31   Damer, Eyre.   When the Ku Klux Rode.   New York: Neale Publishing Company, 1912.

A discussion of the KKK, basically in Alabama, in which the Klan is cited as having "rescued the commonwealth from the control of corrupt adventurers and ignorant freedmen" by establishing an orderly government.

B32   Daniel, James W.   A Maid of the Foot-Hills; or Missing Links in the Story of Reconstruction.   New York: Neale Publishing Company, 1905.

An account of conditions in the post-war South, in

which the activities of the KKK are seen as having helped "severed the shackles which bound the almost helpless populace."

B33 Daniels, Jonathan. Prince of Carpetbaggers. Philadelphia: J. B. Lippincott Company, 1958.

The story of Milton Littlehead, who headed the Union League, and the Klan's activities to oppose him in North Carolina and Florida.

B34 Davis, Daniel S. Struggle for Freedom; The History of Black Americans. New York: Harcourt Brace Jovanovich, 1972.

Passing reference is made to Klan activities during Reconstruction, the 1920s, and the recent civil-rights movement.

B35 Davis, Susan L. Authentic History of the Ku Klux Klan, 1865-1877. New York: American Library Service, 1924.

This sympathetic history of the Klan credits that group with sustaining the policy of white supremacy in the South and maintaining "law and order" despite outrages committed by Freedmen and carpetbaggers.

B36 Degler, Carl N. The Other South; Southern Dissenters in the Nineteenth Century. New York: Harper & Row, Publishers, 1974.

Brief accounts of the efforts of a few southern governors to halt Klan activities in their states.

B37 Desmond, Humphrey J. Curious Chapters in American History. St. Louis: B. Herder Book Co., 1924.

One of the "curious chapters" is the KKK, as a general discussion of its formation, activities, and eventual decline is presented.

B38 Dixon, Edward H. The Terrible Mysteries of the Ku Klux Klan. A Full Expose of the Forms, Objects, and "Dens" of the Secret Order: With a Complete Description of Their Initiation. From the Confession of a Member. New York: M. D. Scalpel, 1868.

A KKK initiation ritual is described in gorey and frightening detail.

B39   Dixon, Thomas, Jr. The Black Hood. New York: Grosset & Dunlap Publishers, 1924.

In this later novel about the KKK, the Klan is seen in the midst of a power struggle between a local Klan leader who feels the KKK is no longer needed to control Radical elements and others who would use the Klan to further their own political or individual plans.

B40   _____. The Clansman; An Historical Romance of the Ku Klux Klan. New York: Grosset & Dunlap Publishers, 1905.

The second and most famous volume of Dixon's KKK trilogy, this novel was the basis of the film Birth of a Nation, which helped the "revived" Klan gain popularity. The KKK is credited with saving the South from the political domination of Freedmen and Radical Republicans and returning the control of local government to conservative Democrats.

B41   _____. The Leopard's Spots; A Romance of the White Man's Burden--1865-1900. New York: Doubleday, Page & Co., 1902.

This first volume of Dixon's trilogy about the KKK deals with post-war life in North Carolina and seeks to reaffirm the principle of white supremacy by glorifying the efforts and principles of the Klan.

B42   _____. The Traitor; A Story of the Fall of the Invisible Empire. New York: Doubleday, Page & Co., 1907.

The third volume of the author's trilogy about the KKK deals with the decline of the "Invisible Empire," whose services are no longer needed as conservative Democrats regain control of the South.

B43   DuBois, W. E. Burghardt. Black Reconstruction; An Essay Toward a History of the Past Which Black Folk Played in the Attempt to Reconstruct Democracy in America, 1860-1880. New York: Russell & Russell, 1935.

The origin and basic activities of the KKK are mentioned, along with glimpses of the Klan's actions in various states.

B44   Dunning, William A.   Reconstruction; Political and Economic, 1865-1877.   Vol. XXII of The American Nation: A History.   Edited by A. B. Hart.   28 vols. New York: Harper & Bros., Publishers, 1907.

This volume contains passing references to the KKK and its activities, and federal legislation aimed at nullifying the Klan.

B45   Evans, W. McKee.   Ballots and Fence Rails; Reconstruction on the Lower Cape Fear.   Chapel Hill: University of North Carolina Press, 1966.

A discussion of KKK activities in the Cape Fear region of North Carolina; especially Klan efforts during the election of 1870, and actions on the part of Republican Governor William Holden to suppress the KKK.

B46   Ezell, John S.   The South Since 1865.   2nd ed.   New York: Macmillan Company, 1975.

The basic principles of the Reconstruction and the "revived" Klan of the '20s are briefly discussed.

B47   Ficklen, John R.   History of Reconstruction in Louisiana, (Through 1868).   Baltimore: Johns Hopkins Press, 1910.

A discussion of the general strength and activities of the KKK throughout the South, with specific examples of Klan activities in Louisiana.

B48   Fleming, Walter L.   Civil War and Reconstruction in Alabama.   New York: Columbia University Press, 1905.

A discussion of the KKK's organization, strength, and activities in Alabama, where it sought to maintain the "supremacy of the white race." Efforts to suppress the Klan are also mentioned.

B49   _____.   Documentary History of Reconstruction; Political, Military, Social, Religious, Educational and Industrial; 1865 to the Present Time. 2 vols. Cleveland: Arthur H. Clark Company, 1906.

Reprints of the "Ku Klux Klan Act" of 1871, the Prescript, or constitution, of the KKK, a number of other Klan documents, testimony of witnesses (both pro and con) from various Klan trials, and the court decision rendering the "Ku Klux Act" unconstitutional are found in this work.

B50   . Documents Relating to Reconstruction. Morgantown, W. Va. : A. G. Strugiss, 1904.

This volume contains a copy of the Prescript, or constitution, of the KKK, a typical threatening Klan order to carpetbaggers, a constitution from a local Klan chapter in South Carolina, and other Klan documents.

B51   . The Sequel of Appomattox; A Chronicle of the Reunion of the States. Vol. XXXII of The Chronicles of America Series. Edited by Allen Johnson. New Haven: Yale University Press, 1919.

A chapter on the KKK describes the organization and some of the activities of the Klan in opposition to the policies of Radical governments throughout the South.

B52 Fletcher, John G. Arkansas. Chapel Hill: University of North Carolina Press, 1947.

A brief discussion of Klan activities in Arkansas and the efforts of Governor Powell Clayton to suppress the KKK is included.

B53 Fry, Gladys-Marie. Night Riders in Black Folk History. Knoxville: University of Tennessee Press, 1975.

An analysis of the origins, dress, and activities of the KKK and the relationship between the Klan and its victims.

B54 Fuller, Edgar I. Nigger in the Woodpile. Lacy, Wash. : Edgar I. Fuller, 1967.

This work, written by a former secretary to Edward Clarke, presents a generalized discussion of the Negro in America and the KKK's relationship to black Americans in both the 19th and 20th centuries. Clarke was one of the advertising people William Simmons employed to publicize the Klan and make it a national organization. When Hiram Evans assumed leadership of the KKK, Clarke was released, and he then wrote a letter to President Calvin Coolidge warning him of the excesses of the Klan. That letter is reprinted in this text.

B55   Gannon, William H.   The G. A. R. vs. the Ku-Klux. A Few Suggestions Submitted for the Consideration of the Business Men and the Working Men of the North. Boston: W. F. Brown & Company, 1872.

B56   Garner, James W.   Reconstruction in Mississippi. New York: Macmillan Company, 1901.

The organization of the KKK in Mississippi, a sampling of the Klan's activities in that state, and the effects of the Ku Klux Klan Act on the Mississippi organizations are presented.

B57   Green, John P.   Recollections of the Inhabitants, Localities, Superstitions and Ku Klux Outrages of the Carolinas.   By a "Carpet-Bagger" Who Was Born and Lived There.   Cleveland: John P. Green, 1880.

A generalized description of KKK activities against Freedmen and carpetbaggers aimed at returning the control of state government to conservative whites.

B58   Green, Paul.   Plough and Furrow; Some Essays and Papers on Life and the Theatre.   New York: Samuel French, 1963.

The author recounts a story about an encounter with the KKK as told to him by an old Negro field hand.

B59   Hamilton, Joseph G. de Roulhac, ed.   The Papers of Randolph Abbott Shotwell.   3 vols.   Vols. II and III. Raleigh: North Carolina Historical Commission, 1931 and 1936.

These papers of a former Confederate officer

and KKK member from South Carolina provide a look at the organization and activities of the Klan in South Carolina and the fate of various Klansmen who were arrested and imprisoned for their deeds, as was the author.

B60   . Reconstruction in North Carolina.   New York: Columbia University Press, 1914.

A description of the KKK in North Carolina, including its organization and membership; numerous examples of Klan activities, which the author sees as being punitive or political in nature; and finally a discussion of the events that lead to the Klan's decline.

B61   Hamilton, Peter J. The Reconstruction Period. Vol. XVI in The History of North America. Edited by Francis N. Thorpe. 19 vols. Philadelphia: George Barrie's Sons, 1905.

A discussion of the origin and activities of the KKK as it sought to maintain the supremacy of the white race in the South and the efforts of federal and state authorities to control the Klan.

B62   Henry, Robert S. The Story of Reconstruction. Indianapolis: Bobbs-Merrill Company, 1938.

A discussion of the organization and activities of the KKK in various southern states.

B63   Horn, Stanley F. Invisible Empire: The Story of the Ku Klux Klan, 1866-71. Boston: Houghton Mifflin Company, 1939.

This history of the KKK traces the development of the post-war organization, its activities in various southern states, its leadership, and the eventual decline of its influence.

B64   Howard, Oliver O. Autobiography of Oliver Otis Howard. 2 vols. New York: Baker & Taylor Company, 1908.

The head of the Freedman's Bureau recounts Klan offenses against Bureau schools and teachers in the

KKK's effort to keep Negroes from obtaining an education.

B65   Howe, Elizabeth M.   "A Ku Klux Uniform. "   Publications of the Buffalo Historical Society.   Edited by Frank H. Severance.   Buffalo, N. Y. :   Buffalo Historical Society, 1921.

The story of a KKK "uniform" from North Carolina and how it came to be housed in the Buffalo Historical Society's museum.

B66   Jones, Robert H.   Disrupted Decades; The Civil War and Reconstruction Years.   New York: Charles Scribner's Sons, 1973.

A brief discussion of the origins, organization, and activities of the Klan, as well as attempts to control the KKK.

B67   Jones, Winfield.   Knights of the Ku Klux Klan.   New York: Tocsin Publishers, 1941.

This volume was written by a former correspondent who was able to obtain permission in the '20s from the then-Imperial Wizard William Simmons to have access to KKK files in researching this book.   While basically a history of the 20th-century Klan, the historical background of the Reconstruction KKK is included, along with profiles of major Klan leaders and reprints of official KKK documents.

B68   Lamson, Peggy.   The Glorius Failure; Black Congressman Robert Brown Elliott and the Reconstruction in South Carolina.   New York: W. W. Norton & Company, ⋏

A discussi✓ of the KKK activities against whites and blacks in South Carolina that led to the convening of the Klan trials in 1871.   This is also one of a few works that does not cite the arming of the Negro militia in South Carolina as the reason for the Klan's appearance.

B69   Lester, John C. , and Daniel L. Wilson.   Ku Klux Klan; Its Origin, Its Growth and Disbandment.   Nashville,

Tenn.: Wheeler, Osborn & Duckworth Manufactur-
ing Co., 1884.

This work, written by one of the original founders
of the KKK and another resident of Pulaski, Tennessee, where the Klan was started, gives a detailed
discussion of the origin of the Klan, how it spread
throughout the South and embarked upon a campaign
to terrorize Negroes and Radical Republicans, and
how it eventually declined and disbanded under pressure of anti-Klan legislation.   A copy of the KKK's
Prescript, or constitution, is included, as well as
other Klan documents.

B70   Let the American People Ponder.   Ku Klux Diabolism.
      Eleven Pregnant Facts Brought to Light by the Con-
      gressional Investigation Committee.   Its Democratic
      Paternity, Its Hellish Features and Party Purpose.
      n. p., 1872.

B71   Lumpkin, Benjamin, defendant.   Full Report of the
      Great Ku-Klux Trial in the U. S. Circuit Court at
      Oxford, Miss.   Memphis, Tenn.: W. J. Mansford,
      1871.

B72   Lynch, James D.   Redpath; or, The Ku Klux Tribunal
      A Poem.   Columbus, Miss.: Excelsior Printing Es-
      tablishment, 1877.

      A poetic tribute to the KKK and its struggle to re-
      turn the control of local government to the conserva-
      tive Democrats of the South.

B73   Madison, Arnold.   Vigilantism in America.   New York:
      Seabury Press, 1973.

      A chapter on the Klan presents a discussion of the
      Reconstruction KKK--how it got started and how it
      developed into a vigilante-type group.   The activities
      of the Klan during the 1920s are also discussed.

B74   The Masked Lady of the White House; or The Ku Klux
      Klan.   Philadelphia: C. W. Alexander, Publisher,
      1868.

      An early fictional account of the KKK involving a
      "masked lady" who had access to the White House.
      While the Klan thought she was helping them to pre-

pare the way to discredit President Andrew Johnson, she was really gathering information to help the Radical Republicans combat the Klan.

B75　Meltzer, Milton. Freedom Comes to Mississippi; The Story of Reconstruction. Chicago: Follett Publishing Company, 1970.

A brief description of the activities of the KKK in Mississippi, including the burning of churches and schools and the forcing of teachers to leave the state.

B76　Memoirs of W. W. Holden. Durham, N. C. : Seeman Printery, 1911.

North Carolina's Radical governor recounts his efforts to control the Klan in his state.

B77　Meriwether, Elizabeth (Avery). The Ku Klux Klan; or The Carpetbagger in New Orleans. Memphis, Tenn. : Southern Baptist Publishing Co. , 1877.

B78　Milner, Duncan C. The Original Ku Klux Klan and Its Successor, A Paper Read at Stated Meeting of the Military Order of the Loyal Legion of the United States, Commandery of the State of Illinois, October 6, 1921, by Companion First Lieutenant and Adjudant Duncan C. Milner, 98th Ohio inf. , U. S. V. Chicago: n. p. , 1921.

B79　Mitchell, George W. The Question Before Congress; A Consideration of the Debates and Final Action by Congress Upon Various Phases of the Race Question in the United States. Philadelphia: A. M. E. Book Concern, 1918.

This work includes a brief analysis of the events leading up to the passage of the Ku Klux Klan Act of 1871.

B80　Monks, William. A History of Southern Missouri and Northern Arkansas; Being an Account of the Early Settlements, the Civil War, the Ku-Klux, and Times of Peace. West Plains, Mo. : West Plains Journal Co. , 1907.

A discussion of KKK activity in Arkansas and along

the Missouri border, and the efforts of Governor Powell Clayton of Arkansas to stop the Klan's acts of violence.

B81 The Nation's Peril. Twelve Years' Experience in the South. Then and Now. The Ku Klux Klan, a Complete Exposition of the Order: Its Purpose, Plans, Operations, Social and Political Significance; the Nation's Salvation. New York: Friends of the Compiler, 1872.

The KKK is seen as a peril to the country; examples of its activities against free Negroes and carpetbaggers are presented. The "nation's salvation" is considered to be the efforts on the part of state and federal officials to combat the Klan.

B82 Oberholtzer, Ellis P. A History of the United States Since the Civil War. 5 vols. Vol. II, 1868-1872. New York: Macmillan Company, 1922.

A chapter on the KKK discusses the formation of the "Invisible Empire"; how it was transformed from an organization aimed at "keeping the free Negroes in their place," by means of outlandish costumes and pranks to scare blacks into submission, into a group seeking to regain control of the reins of state government by means of murder and other acts of violence against Negroes and supporters of Republican rule in the South; and how state and federal authorities sought to control the activities of the Klan.

B83 Osofsky, Gilbert. The Burden of Race; A Documentary History of Negro-White Relations in America. New York: Harper & Row, Publishers, 1967.

This volume contains a reprint of testimony of a KKK victim before a Congressional committee in 1871, an excerpt from William Simmons's views on the Negro as put forth in The Klan Unmasked (see E165), and reports on incidences of Klan violence in Alabama during the early days of the civil-rights movement of the '50s and '60s.

B84 Page, Thomas N. Red Rock; A Chronicle of Reconstruction. New York: Charles Scribner's Sons, 1898.

The Klan is seen as the only resistance to Radical
Republican rule of the South in this novel of the
Reconstruction era.

B85   Patrick, Rembert W.   The Reconstruction of the Na-
      tion. New York: Oxford University Press, 1967.

      A discussion of the KKK's activities and the efforts
      made in various states to control the Klan is pre-
      sented.

B86   Patton, James W.   Unionism and Reconstruction in
      Tennessee, 1860-1869.   Chapel Hill: University of
      North Carolina Press, 1934.

      The KKK's activities in Tennessee are viewed in the
      political context of attempting to keep Negroes from
      voting so conservatives could regain control of state
      government.   Some of the Klan's methods are de-
      scribed, as are the efforts made by Governor Brown-
      low to control the KKK.

B87   Pierson, Hamilton W.   A Letter to Hon. Charles Sum-
      ner, with "Statements" of Outrages upon Freedmen
      in Georgia, and an Account of My Expulsion from
      Andersonville, Ga. , by the Ku Klux Klan.   Washing-
      ton, D. C. :   Chronicle Printers, 1870.

      A report of Klan activity in Georgia from a minister
      and teacher, who was threatened by the KKK and
      forced to leave the South.

B88   Randel, William P.   The Ku Klux Klan: A Century of
      Infamy.   Philadelphia: Chilton Books, 1965.

      In this history of the Klan during Reconstruction and
      in more recent times, the author presents the view
      that the KKK was not a necessary product of the
      Reconstruction era and that its activities are based
      upon a policy of hatred and intolerance.

B89   Raum, Green B.   The Existing Conflict Between Re-
      publican Government and Southern Oligarchy.   Wash-
      ington, D. C. :   Charles M. Greene Printing Co. ,
      1884.

      This work contains a discussion of the KKK, including descriptions of its activities in Louisiana during the elections of 1868; murders and other outrages in Alabama and North and South Carolina; and methods of "encouraging" Negroes to vote Democratic in Georgia. Many of the accounts were taken from testimony given before the Congressional committee investigating the Klan. A copy of the constitution of the KKK is also included.

B90 Report of the Joint Committee on Outrages. Montgomery, Ala.: J. G. Stokes & Co., 1868.

A transcript of testimony given before an investigating committee of the Alabama General Assembly relating to the activities of the Ku Klux Klan in that state.

B91 Reynolds, John S. Reconstruction in South Carolina, 1865-1877. Columbia, S. C.: State Co., Publisher, 1905.

The arming of Negro militia in South Carolina is viewed as the cause of KKK activity within that state, activity that led to a number of murders, the declaration of martial law by U. S. troops, and the eventual Klan trials in Columbia in 1871.

B92 Rhodes, James F. History of the United States from the Compromise of 1850 to the End of the Roosevelt Administration. 9 vols. Vol. VI, 1866-1872. New York: Macmillan Company, 1928.

A discussion of KKK activities throughout the South and a summary of the federal legislation aimed at controlling the Klan are included. Most of the information and examples were taken from testimony given before the Congressional committee investigating the Klan.

B93 Richardson, William T. Historic Pulaski; Birthplace of the Ku Klux Klan. Nashville, Tenn.: Methodist Publishing House, 1913.

A former Klansman attempts to shed some light on the founding of the KKK, its activities in and around the Tennessee community where it was started, and the efforts of Governor Brownlow to put a halt to the KKK.

B94   Romine, William B. A Story of the Original Ku Klux
       Klan. Pulaski, Tenn. : The Pulaski Citizen, 1924.

       A discussion of the original KKK: how it was started
       and by whom, how new members were inducted, and
       how the Klan went from its original purpose to the
       group that began to terrorize Negroes and others
       associated with Radical governments.

B95   Rose, Mrs. S. E. F. The Ku Klux Klan, or Invisible
       Empire. New Orleans: L. Graham Co. , Ltd. , 1914.

       A rather sympathetic history of the KKK by an au-
       thor who views the Klan as an organization that "pre-
       served the purity and domination of the Anglo-Saxon
       race. "

B96   Sefton, James E. The United States Army and Recon-
       struction, 1865-1877. Baton Rouge: Louisiana State
       University Press, 1967.

       A study of the efforts of the U. S. Army in trying
       to suppress the activities of the Ku Klux Klan.

B97   Seitz, Don C. The Dreadful Decade; Detailing Some
       Phases in the History of the United States from Re-
       construction to Resumption, 1869-1879. Indianapolis:
       Bobbs-Merrill Company, 1926.

       A good description of the KKK and some of its ac-
       tivities is provided in the chapter on Reconstruction.
       Included is detailed information about the origins and
       structure of this secret society.

B98   Simkins, Francis B. , and Charles P. Roland. A His-
       tory of the South. 4th ed. New York: Alfred A.
       Knopf, 1972.

       Passing references are made to the Klans of Recon-
       struction and of the '20s and their roles in their re-
       spective societies.

B99   _____, and Robert H. Woody. South Caro-
       lina During Reconstruction. Chapel Hill: Uni-
       versity of North Carolina Press, 1932.

       A description of KKK activities in South Carolina,

predominately in connection with the elections of
1868 and 1870.

B100   Singletary, Otis A.   Negro Militia and Reconstruction.
       Austin: University of Texas Press, 1957.

       A study of the use of Negro militia units, their ac-
       tivities in trying to suppress the KKK, and the Klan's
       reaction to the presence of armed Negroes.

B101   Skaggs, William H.   The South Oligarchy.   New York:
       Devin-Adair Company, 1924.

       A discussion of the formation of the Klan and many
       of its Reconstruction activities, a brief analysis of
       what caused the first Klan's demise, and further
       discussion of the "revived" KKK of the 1920s.

B102   Stearns, Charles.   The Black Man of the South and
       the Rebels.   New York: American News Co., 1872.

       An account of Klan activities as viewed by a North-
       erner residing in Georgia.   The author sees "oppo-
       sition to radical republicanism" as the Klan's sole
       objective.

B103   Sterling, Dorothy, ed.   The Trouble They Seen; Black
       People Tell the Story of Reconstruction.   Garden
       City, N.Y.: Doubleday & Company, 1976.

       This volume contains reprints of newspaper and
       journal articles, personal letters, testimony before
       a Congressional committee, and other sources all
       describing incidents of KKK violence and terrorism
       against southern Negroes.

B104   Swint, Henry L.   The Northern Teacher in the South,
       1862-1870.   New York: Octagon Books, 1967.

       Some of the KKK actions taken against northern
       school teachers helping the Freedman are discussed.

B105   Synnestvedt, Sig.   The White Response to Black Eman-
       cipation; Second-Class Citizenship in the United
       States Since Reconstruction.   New York: Macmillan
       Company, 1972.

The Klan's treatment of Negroes is examined as one form of "white response. " A summary of KKK activities during Reconstruction is included, as is a brief discussion of the more recent murder of three civil-rights workers in Mississippi.

B106   Taylor, Alrutheus A.   The Negro in South Carolina During the Reconstruction.   Washington, D. C. : Association for the Study of Negro Life & History, 1924.

A description of the KKK activities that eventually led to a declaration of martial law over parts of South Carolina and the convening of the Ku Klux Klan trials in Columbia in 1871-72.

B107   _____.   The Negro in Tennessee, 1865-1880.   Washington, D. C. :   Associated Publishers, 1941.

A description of the activities of the KKK in Tennessee and the efforts of Governor Brownlow to keep the Klan in check.

B108   Testimony for the Prosecution in the Case of United States Versus Robert Hayes Mitchell.   Cincinnati: Phonographic Institute Company, 1913.

This volume contains a reproduction of the court reporter's notes of testimony given about KKK activities at the Ku Klux trials in Columbia, S. C. , in 1871.   The testimony given is by witnesses and victims of KKK violence in that state.

B109   Thompson, C. Mildred.   Reconstruction in Georgia; Economic, Social, Political, 1865-72.   New York: Columbia University Press, 1915.

A report on KKK activity in Georgia, including a discussion of where the Klan strength was located within the state, an account of some of the murders committed by the KKK in its effort to regain control of the state government, and the efforts of state authorities to control the activities of the Klan.

B110   Thompson, Henry T.   Ousting the Carpetbagger from South Carolina.   Columbia, S. C. :   R. L. Bryan Co. , 1926.

An account of KKK activities in South Carolina, which were brought about by an increase in crime among Negroes and sought to "frighten the negroes into good behavior. "

B111   Tourgee, Albion W.   A Fool's Errand by One of the Fools.   New York: Fords, Howard, & Hulbert, 1879.

This novel about Reconstruction, written by a Republican judge who resided in the South and sought to bring a halt to the Klan's activities, views the KKK as one of the evils of that era.

B112   _____.   The Invisible Empire: A Concise Review of the Epoch.   Boston: W. H. Thompson & Co. , 1880.

A former judge of the Superior Court of North Carolina, 1868-74, presents his views on the KKK. Tourgee discusses the rise of the Klan and the scope of its activities, giving accounts from both black and white victims.   From having resided in the South during the era, the author is also able to discuss the social background and sentiment that allowed the KKK to start and flourish during Reconstruction.

B113   Trefousee, Hans L.   Reconstruction: America's First Effort at Radical Democracy.   New York: Van Nostrand Reinhold Company, 1971.

The testimony of a Negro resident of South Carolina given before a Congressional investigating committee concerning the activities of the local KKK.

B114   Trelease, Allen W.   White Terror: The Ku Klux Klan Conspiracy and Southern Reconstruction.   New York: Harper & Row, Publishers, 1971.

This history of the KKK during Reconstruction supports the view that the Klan was a white reaction to the new freedom and growing power of southern Negroes and that the idea of white supremacy provided the Klan with the protection it needed to carry out its activities.

B115   Tyler, Charles W.   The K. K. K.   New York: Abbey Press, 1902.

This novel depicts the anxiety and impatience of a community involved with a murder trial. As the trial wears on and the citizens feel that justice is being averted, they turn to a group called the KKK, who hang the accused murderer. Analogies to the activities of the Klan can be easily drawn.

B116   Wiggins, Sarah W. The Scalawag in Alabama Politics, 1865-1881. University: University of Alabama Press, 1977.

An account of the political activities of the Alabama Klans, especially during the election of 1870.

B117   Williamson, Joel. After Slavery; The Negro in South Carolina During Reconstruction, 1861-1877. Chapel Hill: University of North Carolina Press, 1965.

A discussion of the events that led to the "Ku-Klux riots" of 1870-71 in South Carolina. The author sees the arming of Negro militia as a precipitating factor in arousing the KKK to act as a spontaneous reaction, not part of a Klan conspiracy.

B118   Wish, Harvey, ed. Reconstruction in the South, 1865-1877. New York: Farrar, Straus and Giroux, 1965.

This volume contains reprints of material concerning the KKK, including excerpts from testimony of Klan leaders Nathan Forrest and John Gordon and of a victim of Klan violence given before Congressional committees and excerpts from O. O. Howard's autobiography (see B64).

SECTION C: ARTICLES

C1   Alexander, Thomas B. "KuKluxism in Tennessee, 1865-1869." Tennessee Historical Quarterly, VIII (September, 1949), 195-219.

A discussion of the KKK in Tennessee: its origin there and some of its activities aimed at keeping Negroes from voting and at curbing the influence of Radical politicians.

C2   Allen, Frederick L. "KKK." Literary Digest, CXXIV (October, 1937), 15-17.

Reports of Hugo Black's association with the KKK lead many to recall the past deeds of the Klan and what it stands for.

C3   Allen Ward. "A Note on the Origin of the Ku Klux Klan." Tennessee Historical Quarterly, XXIII (June, 1964), 182.

A very brief discussion on the Greek origins of the term Ku Klux Klan.

C4   Arnold, S. G. "Conspiracy of the Ku Klux Klan." Methodist Quarterly, XXXIII (1873), 89.

C5   Bennett, Lerone, Jr. "The First White Blacklash." Ebony, XXII (December, 1967), 146-48+.

As part of a series on the Reconstruction era, this article deals with the KKK's founding and activities, and measures eventually employed to curb it.

C6   Braden, George. "The Ku Klux Klan: An Apology." Southern Bivouac, IV (September, 1885), 103-09.

An attack on D. L. Wilson's Century article (see

37

C52), claiming that the information is inaccurate and Wilson too uncritical of the KKK.

C7   Brown, William G. "Ku Klux Movement. " Atlantic Monthly, LXXXVII (May, 1901), 634-44.

An analysis of the Reconstruction Klan: the conditions that brought it about, what it tried to accomplish, the people who were attracted to it, and the legislative attempts to curb its activities.

C8   Cawein, Madison. "Ku Klux; A Poem. " Chautauquan, LXV (January, 1912), 170.

A poem depicting the "justice" handed out by the KKK.

C9   Cook, Walter H. "Secret Political Societies in the South During the Period of Reconstruction. " Southern Magazine, III (1936), 3-5, 14-17.

A discussion of various organizations that existed in the South during Reconstruction, including information on the organization and activities of the Ku Klux Klan.

C10   Dent, Sanders. "The Origin and Development of the Ku Klux Clan. " Historical Papers of the Trinity College Historical Society, Series I (1897), 10-27.

A discussion of the Klan's beginnings, supporting the idea that the KKK was started solely as a social organization.

C11   Dillon, Merton L. "Captain Jason W. James, Anti-Frontier Democrat. " New Mexico Historical Review, XXXI (April, 1956), 89-101.

The story of a former Confederate officer who joined the KKK during Reconstruction to "save society" and later rejoined the Klan of the '20s to "preserve the Nordic race and the Protestant religion. "

C12   Fleming, Walter L. "A Ku Klux Document. " Mississippi Valley Historical Review, I (March, 1915), 575-78.

Reproduction of the "Ritual" of a KKK group from

Louisiana. The document is basically the induction ceremony for a new Klan member.

C13   _____. "The Prescript of Ku Klux Klan."
Southern History Association, Publications, VII (September, 1903), 327-48.

A reprint of the KKK's Prescript, or constitution, which outlines the organization of the Klan, including its principles, leadership, and symbols.

C14 Gohdes, Clarence. "The Ku Klux Klan and the Classics." Georgia Review, VII (Spring, 1953), 18-24.

A discussion of the derivation of the term "Ku Klux Klan" from the classical languages.

C15 Gregory, Thomas W. "Reconstruction and the Ku Klux Klan." Confederate Veteran, XXIX (August 1, 1921), 292-96.

The KKK is seen as having staged a revolution by overcoming the "unconstitutional" actions of the federal government during Reconstruction.

C16 Gross, Theodore L. "The Negro in the Literature of Reconstruction." Phylon, XX (Spring, 1961), 5-14.

A discussion of Thomas Dixon's portrayal of the KKK in his novels The Leopard's Spots, The Clansman, and The Traitor.

C17 Hall, Andy. "The Ku Klux Klan in Southern Illinois in 1875." Journal of the Illinois State Historical Society, XLVI (Winter, 1953), 363-72.

A discussion of KKK activities in southern Illinois and how local law-enforcement officers attempted to remove the Klan from the area. The Klan re-emerged from the same part of southern Illinois in the 1920s.

C18 Haviland, S. de. "The Ku Klux Klan." Gentleman's Magazine, XL (1887), 436.

C19 Jarvis, Mrs. T. J. "The Conditions That Led to the Ku-Klux Klan." North Carolina Booklet, I (April 10, 1902), 3-24.

C20 _____. "The Ku-Klux Klans." North Carolina Booklet, II (May 10, 1902), 3-26.

This two-part article first discusses the conditions
in North Carolina that gave rise to the KKK in that
state and then describes the organization and activities of the North Carolina Klan.

C21 "The Joke That Became a Terror." Illustrated World,
XXXIII (March, 1920), 110.

A brief article about the origin and purposes of the
original Ku Klux Klan.

C22 Jones, Virgil C. "The Rise and Fall of the Ku Klux
Klan." Civil War Times Illustrated, II (February,
1964), 12-17.

A discussion of the origins of the KKK, its activities, and its eventual disappearance from the scene
as conditions changed in the South.

C23 Kleber, Louis C. "The Ku Klux Klan." History Today, XXI (August, 1971), 567-74.

An analysis of the Reconstruction Klan, including the
origins and early activities of the KKK and how it developed into a terrorist organization aimed at lessen-
ing the control of Republican government in the South.

C24 Krug, Mark M. "On Rewriting the Story of Reconstruction in the U. S. History Textbooks." Journal of
Negro History, XLVI (July, 1961), 133-53.

A discussion of the noncritical and often sympathetic
treatment of the KKK by authors of the history of
Reconstruction.

C25 Lee, Kendrick. "Ku Klux Klan." Editorial Research
Report, II (July 10, 1946), 449-64.

A discussion of the KKK and its activities in three
periods: Reconstruction, the 1920s, and after World
War II.

C26 Lipset, Seymour M. "An Anatomy of the Klan." Commentary, XL (October, 1965), 74-83.

An overview of the KKK, providing some insight into the rises and declines the Klan has experienced in both the 19th and 20th centuries.

C27   McIver, Stuart. "The Murder of a Scalawag. " American History Illustrated, VIII (April, 1973), 12-18.

The story of the murder of John Stephens of North Carolina, as finally revealed by one of the participants.

C28   McNeilly, James H.   "The Enforcement Act of 1871 and the Ku Klux Klan in Mississippi. " Mississippi Historical Society, Publications, IX (1906), 109-71.

C29   _____. "Reconstruction and the Ku-Klux. " Confederate Veteran, XXX (March, 1922), 96-97.

A brief discussion sympathetic to the view that the KKK was started as a reaction to abuses by free Negroes and Radical Republicans.

C30   McWhiney, H. Grady, and Francis B. Simkins. "The Ghostly Legend of the Ku Klux Klan. " Negro History Bulletin, XIV (February, 1951), 109-12.

A discussion of the KKK's use of "ghostly" disguises and how effective they were in frightening Negroes.

C31   Mellard, James M.   "Racism, Formula, and Popular Fiction. " Journal of Popular Culture, V (Summer, 1971), 10-37.

Both Thomas Dixon's The Clansman, depicting the Reconstruction KKK (see B40), and William B. Huie's The Klansman, a modern up-dating of Dixon's work (see E84), are cited as examples of racism in popular fiction.

C32   Mockler, William E.   "The Source of 'Ku Klux. ' " Names, III (March, 1955), 14-18.

A discussion of the derivation of the term "Ku Klux Klan" and how it came to be used when the "Invisible Empire" was originated.

C33   Montgomery, Horace.   "John Buchanan McCormick,

Ballad Singer of Many Talents. " Pennsylvania Magazine of History and Biography, XCII (1968), 239-48.

This article contains the lyrics of McCormick's ballad, "The Ku Klux Klan. "

C34   Olsen, Otto. "The Ku Klux Klan: A Study in Reconstruction Politics and Propaganda. " North Carolina Historical Review, XXXIX (1962), 340-62.

A discussion of KKK activities in North Carolina that questions the interpretation that the Klan was useful in controlling the unlawful abuses of the Radical Republican government.

C35   Pegram, William H. "A Ku Klux Raid and What Came of It. " Historical Papers of the Trinity College Historical Society, Series I (1897), 65-70.

A Klan raid on a North Carolina Negro results in the arrest of 12 suspected Klansmen, including the author; however, no convictions were obtained in the subsequent trial.

C36   Phillips, Paul D. "White Reaction to the Freedmen's Bureau in Tennessee. " Tennessee Historical Quarterly, XXV (Spring, 1966), 50-62.

A report on KKK activities in Tennessee to nullify the presence of the Freedman's Bureau and intimidate Bureau agents.

C37   Post, Louis F. "A 'Carpetbagger' in South Carolina. " Journal of Negro History, X (January, 1925), 10-79.

A Northerner residing in South Carolina during Reconstruction relates his experiences with the KKK and Klan activities in that state.

C38   Reed, J. Walter. "The White Avengers. " Wide World Magazine, XII (December, 1903), 285-92.

A northern school teacher encounters the "White Avengers, " a KKK-type group in Alabama.

C39   Reed, John C. "What I Know of the Ku Klux Klan. " Uncle Remus's Magazine, (January-November, 1908), various paging.

A former KKK member from Georgia relates his experiences with the Klan, presenting his views on why the KKK was started, how it was organized, some of its activities, and reasons for its eventual decline.

C40 Rogers, William W. "Boyd Incident: Black Belt Violence During Reconstruction." Civil War History, XXI (December, 1975), 309-29.

A discussion of KKK activity in Alabama, and its involvement in the murder of Alexander Boyd, Solicitor and Register in Chancery for Greene County, Alabama.

C41 Rose, Mrs. S. E. F. "The Ku Klux Klan and 'The Birth of a Nation.'" Confederate Veteran, XXIV (April, 1916), 157-59.

A discussion of the virtues of the KKK as depicted in the film The Birth of a Nation.

C42 Schaefer, Richard T. "The Ku Klux Klan: Continuity and Change." Phylon, XXXII (Summer, 1971), 143-57.

Three phases of the KKK (the Reconstruction Klan, the "Invisible Empire" of the '20s, and the Klan since the Supreme Court's school-desegregation decision) are examined in relation to two hypotheses: 1) the Klan's targets and tactics have varied with societal changes; and 2) the KKK has developed from a social movement to a mentality.

C43 Shapiro, Herbert. "Afro-American Response to Race Violence During Reconstruction." Science & Society, XXXVI (Summer, 1972), 158-70.

A survey of the black response, which ranged from fight to flight, to the activities of the KKK.

C44 _____. "The Ku Klux Klan During Reconstruction: The South Carolina Episode." Journal of Negro History, XLIX (January, 1964), 34-55.

A discussion of the KKK in South Carolina, its organization, membership and support, its acts, and the reasons for its existence in South Carolina.

C45 Simkins, Francis B. "The Ku Klux Klan in South
     Carolina, 1868-1871. " Journal of Negro History,
     XII (October, 1927), 606-47.

     A study of the extent of, and the motivation behind,
     KKK activities in South Carolina.

C46 Simkins, W. S. "Why the Ku Klux Klan?" Alcalde,
     IV (June 19, 1916), 734-48.

C47 Sloan, John Z. "The Ku Klux Klan and the Alabama
     Election of 1872. " Alabama Review, XVIII (April,
     1965), 113-24.

     The Klan issue is used by Radical Republicans to
     strengthen their control of state government in Ala-
     bama.

C48 Stagg, J. C. A. "The Problem of Klan Violence: The
     South Carolina Up-Country, 1868-1871. " Journal of
     American Studies, VIII (December, 1974), 303-18.

     An analysis of the theories about the conditions in
     South Carolina that gave rise to KKK aggression;
     the author views the Klan in a socioeconomic context.

C49 Swinney, Everette. "Enforcing the Fifteenth Amend-
     ment, 1870-1877. " Journal of Southern History,
     XXVIII (May, 1962), 202-18. (Reprinted in Crowe,
     Charles, ed. The Age of Civil War and Recon-
     struction, 1830-1900; A Book of Interpretive Essays.
     rev. ed. Homewood, Ill. : Dorsey Press, 1975;
     and Hoover, Dwight W. , ed. Understanding Negro
     History. Chicago: Quadrangle Books, 1968.)

     A discussion of how the Enforcement Acts were used
     to combat KKK activities against southern Negroes.

C50 "The Various Shady Lives of the Ku Klux Klan. " Time,
     LXXXV (April 9, 1965), 24-25.

     A very brief history of the KKK from its beginnings
     in Pulaski, Tennessee, up to its activities against
     the recent civil-rights movement in the South.

C51 Wilson, D. L. "The Beginning of the Ku Klux Klan. "
     Southern Bivouac, IV (October, 1885), 269-71.

The author defends earlier remarks he made concerning the origins and history of the KKK against charges that the information was inaccurate.

C52 _____. "The Ku Klux Klan; Its Origin, Growth, and Disbandment." Century Magazine, XXVIII (July, 1884), 398-410.

This article contains excerpts from the Lester and Wilson book on the KKK (see B69).

C53 Wilson, Walter. "The Meridian Massacre of 1871." Crisis, LXXXI (February, 1974), 49-52.

The story of an incident in Meridian, Mississippi, in which Klansmen from Mississippi and Alabama murdered a number of Negroes and anti-Klan Republicans.

C54 Wood, W. D. "The Ku Klux Klan." Texas State Historical Association Quarterly, IX (April, 1906), 262-68.

The author praises the work of the KKK and credits it with preventing "the domination of the Confederate States by the Negro, the humiliation and pauperizing of the Southern whites, and the erection of their territory into solid black Republican satrapies."

C55 Worley, Ted R., ed. "Major Josiah H. Demby's History of Catterson's Militia." Arkansas Historical Quarterly, XVI (Summer, 1957), 203-11.

A report on a militia unit in southern Arkansas that sought to control the activities of the local Klan.

PART II

THE KLAN OF THE 20th CENTURY

SECTION D: DISSERTATIONS, MANUSCRIPTS/ARCHIVES, GOVERNMENT DOCUMENTS

Dissertations

D1   Alexander, Charles C., Jr. "Invisible Empire in the Southwest: The Ku Klux Klan in Texas, Louisiana, Oklahoma, and Arkansas, 1920-1930." Unpublished Ph. D. dissertation, University of Texas, 1962.

    This dissertation was the basis for the author's later work on the KKK (see E2).

D2   Allen, Lee. "The Underwood Presidential Movement of 1924." Unpublished Ph. D. dissertation, University of Pennsylvania, 1955.

D3   Avin, Benjamin H. "The Ku Klux Klan, 1915-1925: A Study in Religious Intolerance." Unpublished Ph. D. dissertation, Georgetown University, 1952.

D4   Birdwhistell, Ira V. "Southern Baptist Perceptions of and Responses to Roman Catholicism, 1917-1972." Unpublished Ph. D. dissertation, Southern Baptist Theological Seminary, 1975.

    A look at the response of Southern Baptists to the anti-Catholicism of the KKK is included in this study.

D5   Bradley, Laura. "Protestant Churches and the Ku Klux Klan in Mississippi During the 1920's." Unpublished M. A. thesis, University of Mississippi, 1962.

D6   Cates, Frank M. "The Ku Klux Klan in Indiana Politics: 1920-1925." Unpublished Ph. D. dissertation, Indiana University, 1971.

    A study of the KKK's power and influence in Indiana, why it attracted so many members from this midwestern state, and how, under the leadership of David Stephenson, it sought to win political control of the state.

D7   Clark, Carter B.   "A History of the Ku Klux Klan in Oklahoma. " Unpublished Ph. D. dissertation, University of Oklahoma, 1976.

A study of the political, social, economic, and cultural factors at work in Oklahoma that led to the second-highest KKK membership of any state in the Union.

D8   Davis, James H.   "The Rise of the Ku Klux Klan in Colorado, 1921-1925. " Unpublished M. A. thesis, University of Denver, 1963.

D9   Davis, John A.   "The Ku Klux Klan in Indiana, 1920-1930: An Historical Study. " Unpublished Ph. D. dissertation, Northwestern University, 1966.

A study of the KKK in Indiana and its effect, especially on education and religion.

D10   Harrell, Kenneth E.   "The Ku Klux Klan in Louisiana, 1920-1930. " Unpublished Ph. D. dissertation, Louisiana State University, 1966.

A study of the power, influence, and activities of the KKK in Louisiana, including the Klan's involvement with the Mer Rouge murders, its venture into the political arena, and its eventual decline.

D11   Howson, Embrey B.   "The Ku Klux Klan in Ohio After World War I. " Unpublished M. A. thesis, Ohio State University, 1951.

D12   Moore, William V.   "A Sheet and a Cross: A Symbolic Analysis of the Ku Klux Klan. " Unpublished Ph. D. dissertation, Tulane University, 1975.

A general description of the KKK, a socioeconomic analysis of its membership, and a content analysis of Klan literature are used in this study to analyze the KKK within a framework of symbolic-status politics.

D13   Moseley, Clement C.   "Invisible Empire: A History of the Ku Klux Klan in Twentieth Century Georgia, 1915-1965. " Unpublished Ph. D. dissertation, University of Georgia, 1968.

This study of the KKK in Georgia deals with its political influence during its heyday in the 1920s, its opposition to organized labor and the "Communist threat" of the '30s and '40s, and its opposition to desegregation and the civil-rights movement of the '50s and '60s.

D14 Snell, William R. "The Ku Klux Klan in Jefferson County, Alabama, 1916-1930. " Unpublished M. A. thesis, Stanford University, 1967.

D15 Toy, Eckard V. , Jr. "The Ku Klux Klan in Oregon; Its Character and Program. " Unpublished M. A. thesis, University of Oregon, 1959.

D16 Weaver, Norman F. "The Knights of the Ku Klux Klan in Wisconsin, Indiana, Ohio, and Michigan. " Unpublished Ph. D. dissertation, University of Wisconsin, 1955.

Manuscript/Archival Collections

D17 Allen, John W. Papers. Special Collections, Morris Library, Southern Illinois University.

This collection contains material on KKK activities in southern Illinois.

D18 Angle, Paul M. Bloody Williamson papers. Manuscript Department, Chicago Historical Society.

A collection of the materials used in researching the book Bloody Williamson (see E7), the author's account of the "war" between law-enforcement officials and the KKK in southern Illinois.

D19 Atwood, Frank E. Papers. Western Historical Manuscript Collection/State Historical Society of Missouri Manuscripts, Ellis Library, University of Missouri.

The papers and records of a candidate endorsed by the KKK for the Missouri Supreme Court.

D20   Bagley, Dudley W.   Papers.   Southern Historical Col-
       lection, Wilson Library, University of North Caro-
       lina.

       The collection contains an invitation to a KKK lec-
       ture in North Carolina in 1925.

D21   Bailey, Josiah W.   Papers.   Manuscript Department,
       Perkins Library, Duke University.

D22   Banta, Edwin P.   Papers.   Manuscripts and Archives
       Division, New York Public Library.

       Correspondence and other material relating to KKK
       activities in Hudson County, New Jersey.

D23   Barnes, Charles M.   Papers.   Western Historical
       Manuscript Collection/State Historical Society of
       Missouri Manuscripts, Ellis Library, University of
       Missouri.

       A description of post-World War I conditions in
       southeast Missouri, including reports of Ku Klux
       Klan activity.

D24   Beittel, Adam D.   Papers.   Historical Collections, Li-
       brary, Talladega College.

       The charter granted to the KKK in 1949 by the state
       of Alabama and correspondence describing Klan activ-
       ity near the campus of Talladega College are con-
       tained in this collection.

D25   Biggers, Don H.   Papers.   Southwest Collection, Li-
       brary, Texas Tech University.

       Correspondence, newspaper clippings, and other ma-
       terial by this Texas journalist, who published an
       anti-Klan newspaper in 1922.

D26   Birger, Charles.   Papers.   Special Collections, Mor-
       ris Library, Southern Illinois University.

       Documents concerning the arrest and execution of
       this Illinois Klansman.

D27   Bowen, Reuben D.   Papers.   Manuscript Department,
       Perkins Library, Duke University.

D28 Brenson, Eugene C. Papers. Southern Historical Collection, Wilson Library, University of North Carolina.

Correspondence concerning KKK activities in North Carolina during 1922-25.

D29 Bruce, John E. Papers. Schomburg Center for Research in Black Culture, New York Public Library.

This collection contains correspondence and editorials relating to the KKK.

D30 Bryan Family. Books and papers. Southern Historical Collection, Wilson Library, University of North Carolina.

Material concerning Charles S. Bryan's membership in the KKK in North Carolina in the early '20s.

D31 Chamberlain, G. Hope. Papers. Manuscript Department, Perkins Library, Duke University.

D32 Christian Advocate. Files. Library, Methodist Publishing House.

A collection of articles about the KKK that appeared in this Methodist newspaper, as well as other Klan-related material from the correspondence and personal files of James R. Joy, editor of the Christian Advocate.

D33 Congress of Industrial Organizations. Organizing Committee. Papers. Manuscript Department, Perkins Library, Duke University.

D34 Craig, Calvin. Interview. Ralph J. Bunche Oral History Collection.

The Grand Dragon of the Georgia KKK discusses the principles and programs of the Klan and gives his views on the race issue (the right to live in harmony among "their class of people").

D35 Cranford, Raymond. Interview. Ralph J. Bunche Oral History Collection.

The transcript of a 1968 interview with a KKK mem-

ber, who gives his opinions on blacks, integration,
poor whites, and contemporary American society.

D36 Davis, William P. Collection. West Virginia Collection, Library, West Virginia University.

Recordings of Klan songs and other KKK memorabilia from the post-World War I era are included in this collection.

D37 Decker, Perl D. Papers. Western Historical Manuscript Collection/State Historical Society of Missouri Manuscripts, Ellis Library, University of Missouri.

Speeches, bulletins, and newspaper clippings concerning Klan activities in Missouri, 1921-24.

D38 Division of Manuscripts. Uncataloged collection. Western History Collections, Monnet Hall, University of Oklahoma.

A photograph of a KKK rally in Bartlesville, Oklahoma.

D39 Edwards, Clark. Papers. Special Collections, Morris Library, Southern Illinois University.

This collection contains a copy of an interview entitled "Dialogue with a Klansman in Jackson County, 1965, " that appeared in a local newspaper.

D40 Edwards, Fredrick C. Papers. Manuscript Department, Perkins Library, Duke University.

D41 Estes, George. Papers. Library, Oregon Historical Society.

Correspondence, papers, and original manuscripts dealing with the KKK in Oregon are included in this collection.

D42 Foulke, William D. Papers. Manuscript Division, Library of Congress.

A collection of mostly anti-Klan material, including newspaper and magazine articles and a copy of a speech by Edgar A. Booth, probably an excerpt from

or the basis of his book The Mad Mullah of America
(see E19).

D43   French, George H.   Papers.   Special Collections, Morris Library, Southern Illinois University.

This collection contains the author's diary for 1925,
which contains references to KKK activities.

D44   Gardner, Paris C.   Papers.   Manuscript Department,
Perkins Library, Duke University.

D45   Glassworkers' Oral History.   West Virginia Collection,
Library, West Virginia University.

A retired West Virginia glassworker recalls some
of the KKK's activities.

D46   Goltra, Edward F.   Papers.   Manuscript Department,
Missouri Historical Society.

This collection contains material concerning the KKK
as a political issue, especially as it affected the
candidacy of John Davis in the 1924 election.

D47   Hamilton, James R.   Papers.   Southern Historical Collection, Wilson Library, University of North Carolina.

Correspondence of a District Court judge in Texas
and his involvement in KKK trials in that state.

D48   Harris, Julian L.   Papers.   Special Collections, Robert
W. Woodruff Library for Advanced Studies, Emory
University.

Information concerning Harris and his editorial
campaign against the KKK in Georgia.

D49   Hinkel, John W.   Papers.   Western Historical Collection, Monnet Hall, University of Oklahoma.

This collection contains material concerning a local
Oklahoma version of the KKK.

D50   Hyde, Arthur M.   Papers.   Western Historical Manuscript Collection/State Historical Society of Missouri
Manuscripts, Ellis Library, University of Missouri.

A number of Klan-related items are contained in
this collection of material from a former governor
of Missouri. The KKK items include material about
the Klan's entrance into Missouri in 1921, popular
reaction to the KKK, Hyde's accusations against
Klan-supported politicians, and former Klansman Hugo
Black's appointment to the Supreme Court.

D51 Jewish Community Relations Council of Minnesota.
Papers. Division of Archives and Manuscripts, Minnesota Historical Society.

A collection of material relating to this group's efforts in opposition to all forms of anti-Semitism, including the activities of the KKK in Minnesota.

D52 Johnston, Henry S. Collection. Western Historical
Collection, Monnet Hall, University of Oklahoma.

A collection of articles and pamphlet material presenting both positive and negative views of the KKK.

D53 Jones, Herbert C. Papers. Special Collections, Library, Stanford University.

This collection contains material in reference to
KKK organizations in Oregon and California.

D54 Kennedy, Stetson. Papers. Schomburg Center for Research in Black Culture, New York Public Library.

The papers of this agent for the Georgia Department
of Law are contained in this collection. Kennedy
wrote two books recounting his experiences with the
KKK and other extremist groups (see E94, E95).

D55 Ku Klux Klan. Broadsides. Manuscript Department,
Chicago Historical Society.

This collection contains one handbill by the Christian
Buyers League to Stop Integration distributed at a
KKK rally near Shreveport, Louisiana, urging buyers
to boycott certain stores and another handbill distributed in Chicago rebutting previous Klan propaganda against Martin Luther King, Jr.

D56 _____. Manuscripts. West Virginia Collection, Library, West Virginia University.

This collection contains the constitution, oaths, membership roster, and other material relating to the KKK in Blacksville, West Virginia.

D57 _____. Materials. Special Collections, Library, Texas A&M University.

This collection contains books dealing with the Klan, as well as annual reports of the Klan, membership cards, sheet music of Klan songs, and other KKK memorabilia.

D58 _____. Miscellaneous materials. Department of Archives and History, State of Georgia.

(See A49.)

D59 _____. Miscellaneous materials. Special Collections, Morris Library, Southern Illinois University.

This collection contains newspaper clippings concerning Klan activities in Williamson and Franklin counties in Illinois.

D60 _____. Miscellaneous materials. Special Collections, Oviatt Library, California State University, Northridge.

A collection of records, papers, pamphlets, and ephemera concerning KKK activities in California, 1922-42.

D61 _____. Papers. Library, Ohio Historical Society.

Letters and other documents relating to attempts in 1924 to establish a statewide KKK organization in Ohio.

D62 _____. Papers. Manuscript Department, Chicago Historical Society.

Correspondence relating to the internal operations of the Indiana Klan during the 1920s.

D63 _____. Papers. Manuscript Department, Perkins Library, Duke University.

D64 _____. Papers. Special Collections, Robert W.

Woodruff Library for Advanced Studies, Emory University.

A collection of records, correspondence, and other material concerning the activities of the Knoxville, Tennessee, KKK in the 1920s.

D65   _____. Records.   Colorado Historical Society.

A collection of material relating to the KKK's presence in Colorado, including a membership roster, brochures, manuals, speeches, and sheet music.

D66   _____. Records.   Oregon Collection, Library, University of Oregon.

A collection of the minutes, financial records, correspondence, and the insignia of the Tillamook chapter of the KKK.

D67   _____. Records.   Texas Collection, Moody Memorial Library, Baylor University.

A collection of material relating to Klan activity in Texas (under the terms of its deposit, this material cannot be opened and described until 1984).

D68 Ku Klux Klan Woman's Organization.   Collection. Western Historical Collection, Monnet Hall, University of Oklahoma.

Correspondence, records, documents, and other material concerning the women's unit of the KKK in Oklahoma.

D69 London, Issac S.   Papers.   Division of Archives and History, North Carolina Department of Cultural Resources.

Material concerning KKK activities in North Carolina is contained in the London papers along with speeches and other comments about the Klan by leading political figures.

D70 Lutheran Church.   Missouri Synod.   Michigan Schools Committee.   Papers.   Michigan Historical Collections, Bentley Historical Library, University of Michigan.

Records of this committee's efforts from 1921 to 1926 to oppose a Klan-inspired constitutional amendment that would ban parochial schools in Michigan.

D71   McGill, Ralph. Papers. Special Collections, Robert W. Woodruff Library for Advanced Studies, Emory University.

The subject files of this journalist contain material about the KKK used in research for various publications.

D72   Mason, Lucy R. Papers. Manuscript Department, Perkins Library, Duke University.

D73   Mencken, Henry L. Papers. Manuscript Department, Perkins Library, Duke University.

D74   Mitchell, Ewing Y., Jr. Papers. Western Historical Manuscript Collection/State Historical Society of Missouri Manuscripts, Ellis Library, University of Missouri.

Material concerning KKK activity in Missouri, especially with regard to the election of 1924.

D75   Mullen Family. Papers. West Virginia Collection, Library, West Virginia University.

Material concerning Dr. A. G. Mullen's membership in the Illinois KKK is contained in this collection.

D76   National Archives. Records.

(See A57.)

D77   National Association for the Advancement of Colored People. Records. Manuscript Division, Library of Congress.

Reports, newspaper clippings, correspondence, and other material concerning KKK activities against Negroes, especially in the areas of voting, housing, and employment.

D78   National Negro Congress. Records. Schomburg Center for Research in Black Culture, New York Public Library.

This collection contains material concerning KKK activities during the Depression and war years, 1933-47.

D79   Nunn, Romulus A.   Papers.   Manuscript Department, Perkins Library, Duke University.

D80   Ogden Family.   Papers.   West Virginia Collection, Library, West Virginia University.

A list of candidates endorsed by the West Virginia KKK in the 1924 elections.

D81   Olcott, Ben W.   Papers.   Oregon Collection, Library, University of Oregon.

Press releases, speeches, and other material concerning the Klan in Oregon can be found in this collection of material from a former governor of the state.

D82   Paisley, Oldham.   Papers.   Special Collections, Morris Library, Southern Illinois University.

The editor of a Marion, Illinois, newspaper recalls KKK activity in that area during the 1920s.

D83   Parker, John M.   Papers.   Southwestern Archives and Manuscripts Collection, Center for Louisiana Studies, University of Southwestern Louisiana.

This collection contains material concerning KKK activities in Louisiana, especially the Mer Rouge murders.

D84   Peterson, H. C. Collection.   Western Historical Collection, Monnet Hall, University of Oklahoma.

This collection contains information about the Knights of Liberty, a Klan-type group in Oklahoma.

D85   Pickens, William.   Papers.   Schomburg Center for Research in Black Culture, New York Public Library.

Correspondence, papers, and newspaper clippings concerning the Ku Klux Klan can be found in this collection from the Field Secretary of the NAACP, 1920-42.

D86 Project South. Transcripts. University Archives, Library, Stanford University.

The transcript of a Klan meeting held in 1966 at Brandon, Mississippi, where Imperial Wizard Robert Shelton was the featured speaker.

D87 Rice, James H., Jr. Papers. Manuscript Department, Perkins Library, Duke University.

D88 Robinson, W. D. Papers. Southern Historical Collection, Wilson Library, University of North Carolina.

Material concerning Klan activities in Louisiana and surrounding states in the early 1920s.

D89 Simms, Robert N. Papers. Manuscript Department, Perkins Library, Duke University.

D90 Slattery, Harry. Papers. Manuscript Department, Perkins Library, Duke University.

D91 Smith, Clarence E. Papers. West Virginia Collection, Library, West Virginia University.

This collection includes newspaper clippings about Klan activities in the area of Fairmont, West Virginia.

D92 Socialist Party of America. Papers. Manuscript Department, Perkins Library, Duke University.

D93 Sweet, William E. Papers. Colorado Historical Society.

Correspondence, speeches, reports, and newspaper clippings by or about this former governor of Colorado, who tried to end the Klan's influence in Colorado politics.

D94 Teagarden, William B. Papers. Barker Texas History Center, Lamar Library, University of Texas.

Correspondence and other material by a Democratic party leader relating to his efforts to increase the party's popularity by opposing the KKK.

D95   Underwood, Oscar W.   Papers.   Southern Historical Collection, Wilson Library, University of North Carolina.

Correspondence concerning KKK activities and its effect on Underwood's political career.

D96   Walton, Jack C.   Collection.   Western Historical Collection, Monnet Hall, University of Oklahoma.

Membership applications, newspaper clippings, and other material concerning the KKK are found in this collection.

D97   Weaver, Carlton.   Collection.   Western Historical Collection, Monnet Hall, University of Oklahoma.

Correspondence concerning Klan activities in Oklahoma during the 1924 election.

D98   Weldon, Bettie.   Collection.   Western Historical Collection, Monnet Hall, University of Oklahoma.

This collection contains photographs of members of the Women of the Ku Klux Klan marching in El Reno, Oklahoma.

D99   Young, Pete.   Interview.   Ralph J. Bunche Oral History Collection.

The transcript of an interview with a newspaper reporter, who views the KKK as a social movement and discusses the socioeconomic plight of the Klan and the gulf between "moderate" and "militant" Klansmen in North Carolina.

Government Documents

D100 U. S. Congress.   House.   Committee on Rules.   The Ku Klux Klan; Hearings Before the Committee on Rules, House of Representatives, Sixty-Seventh Congress, First Session.   Washington, D. C. :   Government Printing Office, 1921.

The testimony of Imperial Wizard Simmons and others before a House investigating committee.   The
testimony concerns the activities of Elizabeth Tyler
and Edward Clarke in promoting and financing the
KKK.

D101   _____.   _____.   Committee on Un-American
Activities.   Activities of Ku Klux Klan Organizations
in the United States, Parts 1-5.   Washington, D. C. :
Government Printing Office, 1966.

The results of HUAC's 1965 investigation of the KKK;
including testimony by Imperial Wizard Robert Shelton and other Klan leaders, examples of official KKK
documents, an examination of Klan financial dealings,
and other activities of the KKK.

D102   _____.   _____.   _____.   Hearings Regarding
H. R. 15678, H. R. 15689, H. R. 15744, H. R. 15754,
and H. R. 16099, Bills to Curb Terrorist Organizations.   Washington, D. C. :   Government Printing
Office, 1966.

The activities of the KKK are discussed in these
hearings before the House Un-American Activities
Committee, which deal with legislation aimed
against the Klan and similar organizations.

D103   _____.   _____.   _____.   The Present-Day Ku
Klux Klan Movement.   Washington, D. C. :   Government Printing Office, 1967.

This report, issued by HUAC after its investigation
of the KKK, deals with the membership, activities,
and leadership of the Klan.   Among the evidence
from the investigation reprinted here are various
charters and official documents of the KKK and a
complete listing of all the existing Klan organizations throughout the country.

SECTION E: MONOGRAPHS

E1   Alexander, Charles C. <u>Crusade for Conformity: The</u> <u>Ku Klux Klan in Texas, 1920-1930.</u> Houston: Texas Gulf Coast Historical Association, 1962.

A study of the KKK's attempts in Texas to enforce a strict moral code on the population, the Klan's involvement in the 1922 senatorial campaign, and the eventual decline of the Klan after its defeat in the 1924 gubernatorial election.

E2   _____. <u>The Ku Klux Klan in the Southwest.</u> Lexington: University of Kentucky Press, 1965.

A discussion of the KKK in the states of the Southwest and its campaign to regulate the patriotic and moral standards of the country.

E3   Allen, Fredrick L. <u>Only Yesterday; An Informal History of the Nineteen-Twenties.</u> New York: Harper & Brothers, Publishers, 1931.

A brief discussion of the Klan's financial situation, as well as its growth and goals during the '20s.

E4   Allstorm, Oliver. <u>The Saddest Story Ever Told.</u> Granite Quarry, N.C.: Knights of the Ku Klux Klan, 1966.

A "poetic" warning against the dangers of interracial marriage.

E5   Alvarez, Joseph A. <u>From Reconstruction to Revolution;</u> <u>The Blacks Struggle for Equality.</u> New York: Atheneum, 1971.

(See B5.)

E6   Anderson, David D. , and Robert L. Wright, eds. The
       Dark and Tangled Race in America.   Boston: Hough-
       ton Mifflin Company, 1971.

       Statements from a KKK attorney defending Alabama
       Klan members for the murder of Viola Liuzzo (see
       F377).

E7   Angle, Paul M.   Bloody Williamson; A Chapter in
       American Lawlessness.   New York: Alfred A.
       Knopf, 1952.

       KKK methods in helping to enforce Prohibition and
       a crackdown on lawbreakers get out-of-hand, and
       open warfare breaks out between Klan and anti-Klan
       forces in the coal-mining region of southern Illinois.
       Only the presence of armed state militia was able
       to end the hostilities.

E8   Barck, Oscar T. , Jr. , and Nelson M. Blake.   Since
       Nineteen Hundred; A History of the United States in
       Our Times.   5th ed.   New York: Macmillan Com-
       pany, 1974.

       Passing references are made to the Klan's anti-
       Catholic, anti-Semitic, and segregationist activities
       in the 20th century.

E9   Bartley, Numan V.   The Rise of Massive Resistance;
       Race and Politics in the South During the 1950's.
       Baton Rouge: Louisiana State University Press, 1969.

       A discussion of the Klan's activities and organization
       in the South during the early civil-rights drive, in-
       cluding Klan attempts to organize southern labor.

E10   Batchelder, M. L. , comp.   Digest of the Laws of the
       Various States Relating to the Ku Klux Klan.   Albany:
       New York State Library, Legislative Reference Sec-
       tion, 1923.

E11   Bates, Daisy.   The Long Shadow of Little Rock; A
       Memoir.   New York: David McKay Company, 1962.

       A recollection of the Klan's role in the attempt to
       stop school desegregation in Arkansas, as told by the
       president of the local NAACP chapter.

E12   Bell, Edward P.   Creed of the Klansmen; Interviews
      with Dr. H. W. Evans, Imperial Wizard of the Ku
      Klux Klan; Israel Zangwill, the Eminent Jewish Au-
      thor; One of the Legal Advisors of the Klan; Mayor
      Ora D. Davis of Terre Haute; Edward H. Morris,
      a Leading Colored Member of the Chicago Bar; and
      Frank Johnston, Jr., Justice of the Illinois Appel-
      late Court.   Chicago: Chicago Daily News Co., 1924.

      The interviewees present their opinions either in
      support or in opposition to the goals and principles
      of the Klan.

E13   Bent, Silas.   Newspaper Crusaders; A Neglected Story.
      New York: McGraw-Hill Book Company, 1939.

      A discussion of various newspapers and their edi-
      torial campaigns against the Klan and its methods.
      The Pulitzer Prize winning articles by the New York
      World are mentioned, along with many others.

E14   Billington, Monroe L.   The Political South in the Twen-
      tieth Century.   New York: Charles Scribner's Sons,
      1975.

      The Klan's political influence during the 1920s is
      seen as an indication of the conservatism in south-
      ern politics.

E15   Black, Earl.   Southern Governors and Civil Rights;
      Racial Segregation as a Campaign Issue in the Sec-
      ond Reconstruction.   Cambridge, Mass.:   Harvard
      University Press, 1976.

      Brief mention is made of the Klan's role in recent
      southern politics, especially in Georgia.

E16   Blake, Aldrich.   The Ku Klux Klan Kraze: A Lecture.
      Oklahoma City: Aldrich Blake, 1924.

      An anti-Klan statement by the executive counselor
      of former Oklahoma Governor John Walton.

E17   Blaustein, Albert P., and Robert L. Zangrando, eds.
      Civil Rights and the American Negro: A Documen-
      tary History.   New York: Trident Press, 1968.

      (See B12.)

E18 Bonner, Thomas N. Our Recent Past; American Civilization in the Twentieth Century. Englewood Cliffs, N. J.: Prentice-Hall, 1963.

A brief analysis of the KKK, its goals and activities during the '20s, and its 1925 march through Washington.

E19 Booth, Edgar A. The Mad Mullah of America. Columbus, Ohio: Boyd Ellison, Publishers, 1927.

The author, a former Klansman, presents his views on the KKK and how leaders like Hiram Evans and David Stephenson turned the Klan into a corrupt political organization, altering the original focus of the order as prescribed by William Simmons, former Imperial Wizard.

E20 Brandfon, Robert L. , ed. The American South in the Twentieth Century. New York: Thomas Y. Crowell Company, 1967.

Reprints of two articles dealing with Miriam Ferguson's election as governor of Texas are included. The first article sets the stage prior to the balloting for either Ferguson or her Klan-supported opponent; the second article provides an analysis of her victory.

E21 Brauer, Carl M. John F. Kennedy and the Second Reconstruction. New York: Columbia University Press, 1977.

A discussion of Klan activities in Alabama and Mississippi as it attempts to interfere with the Freedom Rides and the integration of the University of Alabama, and how disgruntled members of the White Citizens Councils are joining the ranks of the Klan.

E22 Brisbane, Robert H. The Black Vanguard; Origins of the Negro Social Revolution, 1900-1960. Valley Forge, Pa. : Judson Press, 1970.

This work mentions some aspects of the "revived" Klan of the post-World War I era, and a few of the Klan's activities during this 60-year period.

E23 Buni, Andrew. Negro in Virginia Politics, 1902-

1965.   Charlottesville: University Press of Virginia, 1967.

A report on Klan attempts to intervene in the politics of Virginia against regular Democratic candidates.   The KKK was unable to deter support for Al Smith and Harry Byrd, Sr., during the '20s and was also unsuccessful in its support of a conservative candidate for governor in 1965.

E24   Busch, Francis X.   Guilty or Not Guilty?   Indianapolis: Bobbs-Merrill Company, Inc., 1952.

This volume includes a study of the case against Indiana Klan leader D. C. Stephenson for the assault and murder of a young woman.   Stephenson's conviction helped to diminish rapidly the KKK's influence in the Midwest, though the Indiana Klansman claimed he was "framed" by Hiram Evans and the southern wing of the KKK.

E25   Butler, Robert A.   So They Framed Stephenson. Huntington, Ind.:   R. A. Butler, 1940.

E26   Carlson, John R.   The Plotters.   New York: E. P. Dutton & Company, 1946.

A discussion of various right-wing organizations active in the post-World War II years.   The Ku Klux Klan, its leaders, and activities are studied with a discussion of significant Klan organizations in various states.

E27   _____.   Under Cover: My Four Years in the Nazi Underworld of America.   New York: E. P. Dutton & Company, 1943.

A strong connection between the Klan and the German-American Bund and other neo-Nazi groups is shown in this recollection of the author's investigations of these groups.

E28   Cash, William J.   The Mind of the South.   New York: Alfred A. Knopf, 1941.

A brief discussion of the principles of the KKK and how they tied in with the fundamentalist ideology of the 1920s.

E29 Chalmers, David M. Hooded Americanism: The First
Century of the Ku Klux Klan, 1865-1965. Garden
City, N. Y. : Doubleday and Company, 1965.

This volume presents a state-by-state history of the
Klan's activities during the 1920s and beyond, especially the Klan's involvement in the American political scene. A brief discussion of the Klan's Reconstruction origins is also included.

E30 Clark, Thomas D. The Emerging South. 2nd ed.
New York: Oxford University Press, 1968.

The Klan's role in the civil-rights struggle of the
'50s and '60s is discussed, as well as the negative
effects of the KKK on the South's image.

E31 _____, ed. The South Since Reconstruction. Indianapolis: Bobbs-Merrill Company, 1973.

This volume contains a number of reprints concerning the Klan. They include Hiram Evans's speech
Come Now, Let Us Reason Together, remarks condemning the KKK by Luther Hodges and Terry San-
ford, both former governors of North Carolina, and
some anti-Klan articles.

E32 Clark, Thomas D. , and Albert D. Kirwan. The South
Since Appomattox; A Century of Regional Change.
New York: Oxford University Press, 1967.

(See B22.)

E33 Clarke, John H. Marcus Garvey and the Vision of
Africa. New York: Random House, 1974.

This volume contains reprints of interpretive articles
about Marcus Garvey and his Universal Negro Improvement Association. Passing references through
the volume are made to Garvey's statements about
the KKK and his visit with the Imperial Wizard.

E34 Clason, George S. , ed. Catholic, Jew, Ku Klux Klan;
What They Believe, Where They Conflict. Chicago:
Nutshell Publishing Company, 1924.

E35 Clough, Frank C. William Allen White of Emporia.
New York: McGraw-Hill Book Company, 1941.

A discussion of White's 1924 campaign for governor of Kansas on an anti-Klan ticket.

E36   Conkin, Paul, and David Burner. A History of Recent America. New York: Thomas Y. Crowell Company, 1974.

The KKK's resurgence during the 1920s is briefly examined. Also included is a photo of a Klan float in a parade in New Jersey.

E37   Cook, Ezra A. Ku Klux Klan Secrets Exposed; Attitudes Toward Jews, Catholics, Foreigners, and Masons. Fraudulent Methods Used. Atrocities Committed in Name of Order. Chicago: Ezra A. Cook, 1922.

A discussion of the principles of the KKK, how William Simmons organized the Klan, how it recruits its members, and its views on various religious and ethnic groups.

E38   Cook, James G. The Segregationists. New York: Appleton-Century-Crofts, 1962.

Klan growth, membership, and activities since the 1954 school-integration decision are discussed, including information concerning KKK leadership and its future.

E39   Coombs, Norman. The Black Experience in America. New York: Twayne Publishers, 1972.

A brief discussion of the Klan's "revival" during the 1920s is included.

E40   Coughlan, Robert. "Konklave in Kokomo. " The Aspirin Age, 1919-1941. Edited by Isabel Leighton. New York: Simon & Schuster, 1949.

A discussion of the principles and forces behind the KKK of the 1920s. The Klan's development in Indiana is used as an example, as well as a look at the activities of Klan leader David Stephenson.

E41   Cronon, Edmund. D. Black Moses: The Story of Marcus Garvey and the Universal Negro Improvement Asso-

ciation. Madison: University of Wisconsin Press,
1955.

This history of Garvey and the UNIA touches upon
the black leader's relationship with the KKK, and
his highly controversial meeting with the Imperial
Wizard of the Klan.

E42 Curry, LeRoy A. The Ku Klux Klan Under the Search-
light. Kansas City, Md.: Western Baptist Publishing Company, 1924.

A sympathetic view of the Klan and its principles is
presented in this "fair, candid and judicial explana-
tion of Americanism. "

E43 Dabney, Virginius. Liberalism in the South. Chapel
Hill: University of North Carolina Press, 1932.
(Reprinted in Thorp, Willard, ed. A Southern Read-
er. New York: Alfred A. Knopf, 1955.)

A discussion of the Klan's political power and influence and a survey of southern newspapers that opposed the KKK.

E44 Dalrymple, A. V. Liberty Dethroned. Philadelphia:
Times Publishing Co. , 1923.

A condemnation of the Klan by a federal law-enforcement officer, who bases his opinions upon documents
and activities of the KKK.

E45 Davis, Daniel S. Struggle for Freedom; The History
of Black Americans. New York: Harcourt, Brace
Jovanovich, 1972.

(See B34.)

E46 Davis, David B. , ed. The Fear of Conspiracy; Images
of Un-American Subversion from the Revolution to the
Present. Ithaca, N. Y.: Cornell University Press,
1971.

This volume contains material about the KKK from
Paul Winter's What Price Tolerance? (see E191)
and from testimony given during the House Un-
American Activities Committee's investigation of the
Klan.

E47   Dever, Lem A. Masks Off? Confessions of an Im-
       perial Klansman. 2nd ed. , rev. and enl. Portland,
       Ore. : n. p. , 1925.

E48   Drimmer, Melvin, ed. Black History; A Reappraisal.
       Garden City, N. Y. : Doubleday & Company, 1968.

       This work contains excerpts from E. D. Cronon's
       Black Moses: The Story of Marcus Garvey and the
       Universal Negro Improvement Association (see E41),
       dealing with Garvey's relationship with and state-
       ments about the Ku Klux Klan.

E49   Duffus, Robert L. "The Ku Klux Klan at Work. "
       Their Majesties the Mob. Edited by John W. Cau-
       chey. Chicago: University of Chicago Press, 1960.

       An account of a 1922 incident in which two men
       were murdered by the Klan in Mer Rouge, Louisiana.

E50   Elovitz, Mark H. A Century of Jewish Life in Dixie:
       The Birmingham Experience. University: University
       of Alabama Press, 1974.

       A brief discussion of the KKK's strength and influ-
       ence in Birmingham, Alabama, and how it affected
       Jewish residents of that city.

E51   Estes, George. The Roman Katholic Kingdom and the
       Ku Klux Klan. Troutdale, Ore. : Geo. Estes, 1923.

       This anti-Catholic tract views the strength and dom-
       inance of the Catholic Church as dangerous and un-
       American, especially in its efforts in opposition to
       the KKK.

E52   Evans, Hiram W. The Klan Answers ... What the
       Klan Has Done, What the Klan Must Do, Why the
       Klan Is Needed, Why We Are Klansmen. Atlanta:
       American Printing and Manufacturing Co. , 1929.

E53   _____ . The Klan of Tomorrow and the Klan Spir-
       itual. Kansas City, Mo. : Knights of the Ku Klux
       Klan, Inc. , 1924.

       Imperial Wizard Hiram W. Evans speaks of the
       Klan's desire to promote "nationalism" and of some

of the forces working against this principle in an address before the 1924 Imperial Klonvokation.

E54   . The Menace of Modern Immigration. Dallas: n. p. , 1923.

The Imperial Wizard cites statistics concerning illiteracy, disease, and poor housing conditions among recent immigrants as he presents the Klan's anti-alien views.

E55   . The Public School Problem in America; Outlining Fully the Policies and the Program of the Knights of the Ku Klux Klan Toward the Public School System. n. p. , 1924.

E56 Ezell, John S. The South Since 1865. New York: Macmillan Company, 1963.

(See B46.)

E57 Fax, Elton C. Garvey; The Story of a Pioneer Black Nationalist. New York: Dodd, Mead & Company, 1972.

The story of the head of the Universal Negro Improvement Association and his "alleged union" with the KKK.

E58 Fellman, David. The Constitutional Right of Association. Chicago: University of Chicago Press, 1963.

A discussion of various anti-Klan laws passed in several states and the legal interpretations of those laws.

E59 Fleming, John S. What Is Ku Kluxism?; Let Americans Answer--Aliens Only Muddy the Waters. Birmingham, Ala. : Masonic Weekly Recorder, 1923.

A defense of the Klan and its principles of "100% Americanism" and opposition to immigration, especially by Catholics.

E60 Forster, Arnold. A Measure of Freedom. Garden City, N. Y. : Doubleday & Company, 1950.

In this report on recent incidences of anti-Semitism, a chapter is devoted to Klan activities in the post-World War II years.

E61 _____, and Benjamin R. Epstein. The New Anti-Semitism. New York: McGraw-Hill Book Company, 1974.

A brief discussion of the Klan and its organization since 1954 is included.

E62 _____. Report on the Ku Klux Klan. New York: Anti-Defamation League of B'nai B'rith, 1965.

A look at the leadership and activities of the contemporary KKK, including a chronology of Klan activities in the early '60s.

E63 _____. The Troublemakers. Garden City, N. Y.: Doubleday & Company, 1952.

A number of references are made to examples of the Klan's anti-Semitic activities in this report, prepared at the request of the Anti-Defamation League.

E64 Frost, Stanley. The Challenge of the Klan. Indianapolis: Bobbs-Merrill Company, 1924.

A look at the Klan of the '20s. While some of the material was taken from articles the author wrote for Outlook, a considerable amount of new material was added. The goals and leadership of the KKK are discussed, and an attempt to analyze the Klan from a religious viewpoint is made. The appendix contains a copy of the constitution of the Ku Klux Klan.

E65 Fry, Henry P. The Modern Ku Klux Klan. Boston: Small, Maynard & Co., 1922.

A former Klansman "exposes" the anti-Negro, anti-Catholic, anti-Semitic, and anti-foreigner purposes of the KKK. The work contains a number of quotes by Klan leaders, including Imperial Wizard William J. Simmons, and excerpts from various newspapers across the country, especially from the series of articles by the New York World, and from official

KKK publications concerning the activities of the Klan.

E66   Fuller, Edgar I.   The Ku Klux Bubble.   Omaha: M. E. Jacobs and L. B. Bozell, 1923.

E67   _____.   Nigger in the Woodpile.   Lacey, Wash.: Edgar I. Fuller, 1967.

(See B54.)

E68   _____.   The Visible of the Invisible Empire, "The Maelstrom." rev. and ed. by George La Dura. Denver: Maelstrom Publishing Company, 1925.

E69   Gillette, George A.   Dr. Ku Klux Questioned; A Consideration of Crime Contagion and the Klan Cure. Springfield, Mo.:   Geo. A. Gillette, 1925.

A discussion of the idea that by employing the Klan's principles of "100% Americanism," organized crime and the gouging of the average citizen by big crime bosses can be eliminated.   The author, however, feels that the KKK's means don't justify their ends, and that a dictator in a sheet urging "Americanism" is as bad as any Czar that ruled Russia.

E70   Gillette, Paul J.   Ku Klux Klan; The Invisible Empire. New York: Natlus Publications, 1964.

E71   _____, and Eugene Tillinger.   Inside Ku Klux Klan.   New York: Pyramid Books, 1965.

E72   Gillis, James M.   The Ku Klux Klan.   New York: Paulist Press, 1922.

This tract makes light of the KKK and its penchant for inflated titles, regalia, and the like, but it ends with a warning that the Klan should be taken seriously and steps should be taken to curb this potential menace.

E73   Glock, Charles Y., and Ellen Siegelman, eds.   Prejudice, U. S. A.   New York: Frederick A. Praeger, Publishers, 1969.

This volume includes a brief discussion of the KKK

as an exponent of various prejudices during the 1920s.

E74 Goodman, Walter. The Committee; the Extraordinary Career of the House Committee on Un-American Activities. New York: Farrar, Straus and Giroux, 1968.

Some insight into HUAC's 1966 investigation of the Ku Klux Klan is provided.

E75 Greene, Ward. Star Reporters and 34 of Their Stories. New York: Random House, 1948.

Excerpts from the New York World's expose of the KKK are included.

E76 Gunther, Lenworth, ed. Black Image; European Eyewitness Accounts of Afro-American Life. Port Washington, N.Y.: Kennikat Press, 1978.

This volume includes a reprint of an interview with Robert Shelton, Grand Wizard of the Klan, that appeared in an Australian newspaper.

E77 Haas, Ben. KKK. Evanston, Ill.: Regency Books, 1963.

E78 Haldeman-Julius, Emanuel. K. K. K.; The Kreed of the Klansmen. Girard, Kan.: Haldeman-Julius Co., 1924.

E79 Hamilton, Virginia V. Hugo Black; The Alabama Years. Baton Rouge: Louisiana State University Press, 1972.

A study of the power and influence the KKK held in Alabama during the '20s and the relationship between Hugo Black and the Klan organization.

E80 Higham, John. Strangers in the Land; Patterns of American Nativism, 1860-1925. New Brunswick, N. J.: Rutgers University Press, 1955.

A discussion of the Klan's activities during the 1920s, especially against Catholic and Jewish immigrants.

E81 Hinshaw, David. A Man from Kansas; The Story of
William Allen White. New York: G. P. Putnam's
Sons, 1945.

A discussion of White's editorial and political campaigns against the activities of the Ku Klux Klan in
Kansas.

E82 Hofstadter, Richard. The Age of Reform; From Bryan
to F. D. R. New York: Alfred A. Knopf, 1955.

A brief discussion of the KKK as a protector of the
nation's morals, opposing the vices of urban life
and the people who live there.

E83 Hohenberg, John, ed. The Pulitzer Prize Story.
New York: Columbia University Press, 1959.

This volume contains excerpts from Pulitzer Prize
winning articles that opposed the KKK and its activities.

E84 Huie, William B. The Klansman. New York: Dela-
corte Press, 1967.

This novel, set in Alabama in the mid-'60s, depicts
how the KKK can, through support of the local
"power elite," come to have a significant impact on
the lives of moderate white, as well as black, residents of a community.

E85 _____. Three Lives for Mississippi. New York:
WCC Books, 1965.

The story of the three civil-rights workers, Goodman,
Chaney, and Schwerner, who were killed by the KKK
in Mississippi.

E86 Illinois General Assembly. Legislative Investigating
Commission. Ku Klux Klan; A Report to the Illinois
General Assembly. Chicago: The Commission,
1976.

A report on contemporary KKK organization and activities in Illinois. Also included is some background material on the Klan's historical development,
as well as reprints of some official Klan documents.

E87   The Inglewood Raiders; Story of the Celebrated Ku Klux
        Case at Los Angeles and Speeches to the Jury.   Los
        Angeles: L. L. Bryson, 1923.

        The story of a "raid" by Klan members against a
        couple of "bootleggers" in the Los Angeles area in
        1922.   The raiders were taken to trial and the text
        of some of the arguments presented to the jury by
        both the prosecution and defense are included.

E88   Is the Ku Klux Klan Constructive or Destructive?; A
        Debate Between Imperial Wizard Evans, Israel Zang-
        will and Others.   Girard, Kan.:   Haldeman-Julius
        Company, 1924.

        Imperial Wizard Evans discusses the principles of
        the KKK in an interview with correspondent Edward
        Bell of the Chicago Daily News.   Israel Zangwill
        counters Evans's arguments, especially those concern-
        ing the unassimilability of Jewish and Catholic immi-
        grants.   Also included are statements by Klan lead-
        ers from Indiana, an anti-Klan gubernatorial candi-
        date also from Indiana, and a prominent Negro at-
        torney from Chicago.

E89   Jackson, Kenneth T.   The Ku Klux Klan in the City,
        1915-1930.   New York: Oxford University Press,
        1967.

        The idea that the KKK was a rural organization is
        attacked in this discussion of the Klan's strength and
        influence in urban areas.

E90   Jefferson, Charles E.   Five Present-Day Controversies.
        New York: Fleming H. Revell Company, 1924.

        In this volume of five sermons preached by a Prot-
        estant minister in New York, the last section, "Ro-
        man Catholicism and the Ku Klux Klan," attempts
        to explain the dichotomy between the KKK and the
        Catholic Church.   The author feels that the Klan
        does not oppose the religious principles or cere-
        monies of Catholicism, but instead is against the
        hierarchical form of government that controls the
        Catholic Church.

E91   Johnsen, Julia E., comp.   Ku Klux Klan.   New York:
        H. W. Wilson Company, 1924.

A short bibliography of material concerning the KKK
and reprints of selected articles both defending and
attacking the Klan.

E92 Johnson, Walter.   William Allen White's America.   New
York: Henry Holt and Company, 1947.

A discussion of Kansas newsman William Allen White
and his anti-Klan stance, including his campaign for
governor in 1924 in opposition to the KKK.

E93 Jones, Winfield.   Knights of the Ku Klux Klan.   New
York: Tocsin Publishers, 1941.

(See B67.)

E94 Kennedy, Stetson.   I Rode with the Ku Klux Klan.
London: Arco Publishers, Limited, 1954.

The activities of the KKK in Georgia and other parts
of the South are recalled by a Klan infiltrator working for the Georgia Attorney-General's office.

E95 _____.   Southern Exposure.   Garden City, N. Y. :
Doubleday & Company, 1946.

A discussion of KKK organization and activities, especially the years prior to, during, and immediately
after World War II.   Included is a sample applica-
tion for "citizenship in the Invisible Empire" and
other Klan documents and a discussion of the Klan's
relations with organized labor in the South.

E96 Kent, Frank R.   The Democratic Party; A History.
New York: Century Co. , 1928.

A brief discussion of the Klan issue during the 1924
Democratic national convention and the KKK's support of William McAdoo in the Presidential campaign.

E97 Kent, Grady R.   Flogged by the Ku Klux Klan.   Cleveland, Tenn. :   White Wing Publishing House, 1942.

E98 The K. K. K. Katechism; Pertinent Question, Pointed
Answers.   Columbus, Ohio: Patriot Publishing Co. ,
1924.

E99 The Klan in Action; A Manual of Leadership for Offi-

cers of Local Klans.   Atlanta: American Printing
and Mfg. Co. , 1922.

This small pamphlet is a guide on how to operate
a local Klan, giving policy and procedures on such
topics as leadership, essential policies, agenda for
a business meeting, responsibilities of officers, and
a breakdown of necessary committees and their
duties.

E100   Kruszka, Peter P. You Wouldn't Believe It.   Chicago:
Brafman Publishers, 1939.

A northern doctor encounters the KKK during a
journey in Florida.

E101   Ku Klux Klan. Constitution and Laws of the Knights
of the Ku Klux Klan.   Atlanta: Knights of the Ku
Klux Klan, 1921.

The KKK presents its official statement as to its
principles and organization, including officers and
their duties, membership regalia, local Klans,
revenues, and more, in its constitution.

E102   _____. Klansman's Manual.   Atlanta: Buckhead,
1924.

Another version of the Klan's organization, govern-
ance, ritual, creed, leadership duties, etc. , of
both the national and local KKK units.

E103   _____. K of K vs. K of C; Knights of the Klan
Versus Knights of Columbus.   Oklahoma City:
Reno Publishing Co. , 1924.

This KKK-inspired pamphlet depicts the Klan as a
bulwark against a Catholic takeover of our government, school systems, institutions, and such and
subjugation of the country to the Pope.

E104   _____. Papers Read at the Meeting of Grand Dra-
gons, Knights of the Ku Klux Klan at Their First
Annual Meeting Held at Asheville, North Carolina,
July, 1923. n. p. , n. d.

This collection of speeches and essays delivered at

a meeting of KKK leaders includes Imperial Wizard
Evans's views on where the Klan should direct its
efforts; the Klan's attitude toward both Catholics
and Jews, as presented by Evans; and other items
of interest to Klansmen, such as a statement of the
Klan's principles and purposes, and how to operate
a model KKK realm.

E105 The Ku Klux Klan; Official, Unofficial and Anti-Klan
Sources. New York: Andronicus Publishing Company, 1977.

E106 Lamon, Lester C. Black Tennesseans, 1900-1930.
Knoxville: University of Tennessee Press, 1977.

A look at the KKK in Tennessee during the first
30 years of the century. The black vote is seen
as crucial to defeating various Klan political candidates.

E107 Lerner, Max. Actions and Passions; Notes on the
Multiple Revolution of Our Time. New York: Simon & Schuster, 1949.

A brief description of the rise of the "revived"
KKK under William Simmons is included.

E108 Leuchtenburg, William E., ed. The Unfinished Century; America Since 1900. Boston: Little, Brown
and Company, 1973.

A brief discussion of the growth of the KKK and
its attitudes toward minority groups and public
morality.

E109 Levinger, Lee J. Anti-Semitism in the United States;
Its History and Causes. New York: Bloch Publishing Co., 1925.

A discussion of the KKK theory that the Jew is un-
assimilable and seeks to remain within a closed
society, which justifies the principle of restricting
Klan membership to native-born gentiles who accept the tenets of the Christian religion.

E110 Likins, William M. Patriotism Capitalized or Religion Turned into Gold. Uniontown, Pa.: Watch-
man Publishing Company, 1925.

The author, a former Klansman, sees the KKK as entirely divorced from the Protestant church, and that the "Invisible Empire" is using the name of Christianity to sell memberships.

E111 _____. The Trail of the Serpent. Uniontown, Pa.: n. p., 1928.

E112 Lipset, Seymour M., and Earl Raab. The Politics of Unreason; Right-Wing Extremism in America, 1790-1970. New York: Harper & Row, Publishers, 1970.

In this discussion of the KKK as an extremist group, the appeal and support of the Klan of the '20s is analyzed, as is the 1960s-style KKK. The appeal of the more recent Klan is compared with the appeal of the George Wallace movement.

E113 Loucks, Emerson H. The Ku Klux Klan in Pennsylvania; A Study in Nativism. New York: Telegraph Press, 1936.

A study of the KKK's strength and activities in Pennsylvania, being representative of the Klan's appeal in the Northeast.

E114 Lougher, E. H. The Kall of the Klan in Kentucky. Greenfield, Ind.: W. Mitchell Printing Company, 1924.

E115 Lowe, David. Ku Klux Klan: The Invisible Empire. New York: W. W. Norton & Company, 1967.

Lowe was the writer/producer of the 1965 CBS Reports program from which this book draws its title. This volume is basically the text of that program, which dealt with the KKK of the '60s and its involvement in the civil-rights movement. Interviews with various Klan leaders are included, and the many photographs give a good picture of the people who make up the Ku Klux Klan.

E116 McBee, William D. The Oklahoma Revolution. Oklahoma City: Modern Publishers, 1956.

An account of the situation in Oklahoma during the

1920s that saw Governor John Walton declare mar-
tial law in parts of the state to combat KKK forces.
The author was the Speaker of the state House of
Representatives during the period discussed.

E117   McCord, William.   Mississippi: The Long, Hot Sum-
       mer.   New York: W. W. Norton & Company, 1965.

       A discussion of Klan activities to deter civl-rights
       workers in Mississippi during the summer of 1964.

E118   McCorvey, Thomas C.   "The Invisible Empire." Ala-
       bama Historical Sketches.   Edited by George B.
       Johnston.   Charlottesville: University of Virginia
       Press, 1960.

       A description of the organization and early activ-
       ities of the KKK is presented in this sympathetic
       treatment of the Klan.

E119   McGill, Ralph.   The South and the Southerner.   Bos-
       ton: Little,   Brown and Company, 1963.

       A brief survey of the fortunes of the KKK and its
       leadership from the '20s to the desegregation strug-
       gle of the 1950s.

E120   McIlhany, William H.   Klandestine; The Untold Story
       of Delmar Dennis and His Role in the FBI's War
       Against the Ku Klux Klan.   New Rochelle, N. Y. :
       Arlington House, Publishers, 1975.

       An informer for the FBI provides evidence that leads
       to the arrest and conviction of Mississippi Klansmen
       for the murder of three civil-rights workers.

E121   McReynolds, Edwin C.   Oklahoma; A History of the
       Sooner State.   Norman: University of Oklahoma
       Press, 1954.

       A very brief discussion of the impeachment of
       Oklahoma's Governor John C. Walton for abusing
       his powers in his opposition to the Klan.

E122   Madison, Arnold.   Vigilantism in America.   New York:
       Seabury Press, 1973.

       (See B73.)

E123   Manchester, William. The Glory and the Dream: A
        Narrative History of America, 1932-1972. Boston:
        Little, Brown and Company, 1973.

        A brief discussion of the KKK's activities in oppo-
        sition to the civil-rights movement of the 1960s.

E124   Mars, Florence. Witness in Philadelphia. Baton
        Rouge: Louisiana State University Press, 1977.

        A resident of Philadelphia, Mississippi, recounts
        the events surrounding the murder of three civil-
        rights workers there, the FBI's investigation and
        discovery of the bodies, and the trial of 18 Klan
        members for those murders. The author, who
        testified before a grand jury investigating the mur-
        ders, was ostracized by the KKK and became an
        outcast in the community where she grew up.

E125   The Martyred Klansman in Which Events Leading Up
        to the Shooting Death of Klansman Thomas Rankin
        Abbott on August 25, 1923, Are Related, Together
        with a Record of the Court Proceedings That Fol-
        lowed. Pittsburgh: Patriotic American Publishing
        Co. , 1923.

E126   Mast, Blaine. K. K. K. , Friend or Foe: Which?
        Pittsburgh: Herbrick & Held Printing Co. , 1924.

E127   Mecklin, John M. The Ku Klux Klan: A Study of the
        American Mind. New York: Harcourt, Brace and
        Company, 1924.

        This volume was one of the first attempts to ana-
        lyze the appeal of the Klan by looking at the people
        who joined it.

E128   Mendelsohn, Jack. The Martyrs; Sixteen Who Gave
        Their Lives for Racial Justice. New York: Harper
        & Row, Publishers, 1966.

        The Klan's involvement in the death of various
        civil-rights workers, including Viola Liuzzo;
        Schwerner, Goodman, and Chaney; and others.

E129   Miller, Robert M. "The Ku Klux Klan. " Change and
        Continuity in Twentieth-Century America: The 1920's.

Edited by John Braeman, Robert H. Bremer, and David Brody. Columbus: Ohio State University Press, 1968.

An analysis of conditions that led to the KKK's "revival" during the '20s, the principles upon which the Klan based its growth, its organization, activities, and eventual decline.

E130 Milner, Duncan C. The Original Ku Klux K an and Its Successor, A Paper Read at Stated Meeti..g of the Military Order of the Loyal Legion of the Unite⁻ States Commandery of the State of Illinois, O ·t.ber 6, 1921, by Companion First Lieutenant and Ｌdju-tant Duncan C. Milner, 98th Ohio inf., U. S. V. Chicago: n. p., 1921.

E131 Monteval, Marion. The Klan Inside Out. Claremore, Okla.: Monarch Publishing Co., 1924.

A discussion of the beginnings of the 20th-century Klan by William Simmons (with help from Edward Clarke and Elizabeth Tyler), the rise of Hiram Evans, and the corruption of the KKK's original principles as the "Invisible Empire" grew larger and began using intimidation and force to ensure its political control in some areas. Copies of various Klan documents are also included.

E132 Moore, Edmund A. A Catholic Runs for President; The Campaign of 1928. New York: Ronald Press Company, 1956.

A discussion of the KKK's anti-Catholic and anti-urban principles and how they were directed toward Al Smith during his 1928 Presidential campaign.

E133 Moore, Powell A. The Calumet Region; Indiana's Last Frontier. Indianapolis: Indiana Historical Bureau, 1959.

A discussion of the Klan's influence and activities in this area of northern Indiana.

E134 Muse, Benjamin. Ten Years of Prelude; The Story of Integration Since the Supreme Court's 1954 Decision. New York: Viking Press, 1964.

The author credits the 1954 Supreme Court's school-desegregation decision with giving new life to a dying KKK in the South. Examples of Klan activities in trying to thwart desegregation attempts are included.

E135   Myers, Gustavus. History of Bigotry in the United States. New York: Random House, 1943.

Three chapters of Myers's History deal with the KKK of the 1920s. The material deals with the rebirth of the Klan in the South, its spread throughout the country, and its eventual decline.

E136   Myrdal, Gunnar. An American Dilemma; The Negro Problem and Modern Democracy. New York: Harper & Brothers, Publishers, 1944.

A number of passing references are made to the KKK as an example of an anti-Negro group.

E137   Nash, Gary B. , and Richard Weiss, eds. The Great Fear; Race in the Mind of America. New York: Holt, Rinehart and Winston, 1970.

A section on the KKK discusses the conditions that gave rise to the Klan during the '20s and the reception it received in major cities like New York, Boston, and Chicago.

E138   Official Report of the Proceedings of the Democratic National Convention Held in Madison Square Garden, New York City, June 24, 25, 26, 27, 28, 29, 30, July 1, 2, 3, 4, 5, 6, 7, 8, and 9, 1924, Resulting in the Nomination of John W. Davis (of West Virginia) for President and Charles W. Bryan (of Nebraska) for Vice-President. Indianapolis: Bookwalter-Ball-Greathouse Printing Co. , 1924.

The official transcript of the 1924 Democratic national convention, where the delegates were unable to pass a resolution in opposition to the Ku Klux Klan.

E139   Osofsky, Gilbert. The Burden of Race; A Documentary History of Negro-White Relations in America. New York: Harper & Row, Publishers, 1967.

(See B83.)

E140 Peirce, Neal R. The Deep South States of America; People, Politics, and Power in the Seven Deep South States. New York: W. W. Norton & Company, 1972.

A number of references are made to the strength and activities of the KKK during the 1950s and '60s in Alabama, Florida, Georgia, Louisiana, Mississippi, and South Carolina.

E141 Percy, William A. Lanterns on the Levee; Recollections of a Planter's Son. New York: Alfred A. Knopf, 1941.

The author recounts his early experiences with, and his father's opposition to, the KKK's anti-Catholicism in Mississippi.

E142 Powell, Luther I. "The Ku Klux Klan and the Public Schools." The Old Cedar School. George Estes. Troutdale, Ore.: Geo. Estes, 1922.

The introduction to this tract is by the head of the KKK in Oregon; it discusses the Klan's crusade for mandatory public education against the "encroachment of private schools," basically Catholic institutions. The work by Estes lauds public education.

E143 Quint, Howard H. Profile in Black and White; A Frank Portrait of South Carolina. Washington, D. C.: Public Affairs Press, 1958.

A brief discussion of the KKK in South Carolina and its efforts to oppose racial desegregation in the early 1950s.

E144 Randel, William P. The Ku Klux Klan: A Century of Infamy. Philadelphia: Chilton Books, 1965.

(See B88.)

E145 Rauch, Joseph. The Ku Klux Klan; An Examination of Their Theories of White, Protestant and Native. Louisville, Ky.: n. p., 1923.

This collection of three sermons preached by a Louisville rabbi examines the Klan's principle of the supremacy of native-born, white, Protestant Americans.

E146   Reimers, David M.   White Protestantism and the
        Negro.   New York: Oxford University Press, 1965.

        Brief comments about the relationship between
        Protestant churches and the KKK during the '20s.

E147   Rice, Arnold S.   The Ku Klux Klan in American Poli-
        tics.   Washington, D. C. :   Public Affairs Press,
        1962.

        This study traces the KKK's growth and develop-
        ment as a political influence since 1915, with a
        major emphasis on the Klan's role in southern
        politics during the 1920s.

E148   Rogers, John.   The Murders of Mer Rouge.   St.
        Louis: Security Publishing Co. , 1923.

E149   Rosenstock, Morton.   Louis Marshall, Defender of
        Jewish Rights.   Detroit: Wayne State University
        Press, 1965.

        The anti-Semitic activities of the Klan are discussed
        in this work about a prominent Jewish spokesman of
        the '20s, who felt the KKK was a Protestant issue
        and should be handled by that group, urging Jews
        to take a position of cautious inaction.

E150   Rosenthal, A. M. , and Arthur Gelb.   One More Vic-
        tim.   New York: New American Library, 1967.

        The story of a young man of Jewish descent, who
        was a member of both the American Nazi party
        and the Ku Klux Klan.

E151   Roy, Ralph L.   Apostles of Discord; A Study of Or-
        ganized Bigotry and Disruption on the Fringes of
        Protestantism.   Boston: Beacon Press, 1953.

        A discussion of the KKK from a religious perspec-
        tive.   The Klan's activities in the name of "Prot-
        estant morality" are called "a facade for unethical
        practices. "   A look at religious leaders associated
        with the Klan is included.

E152   Rubin, Victor.   Tar and Feathers.   Chicago: Uni-
        versal Press, 1923.

A wounded American soldier, pulled from a European battlefield by a Negro soldier and healed by a Jewish surgeon, returns to his native South following World War I and joins the Ku Klux Klan in this novel depicting the racial and religious prejudices of the KKK during the 1920s.

E153 Russo, Pasquale. Ku Klux Klan; Church and Labor. Chicago: P. Russo, 1923.

E154 Sawyer, Reuben H. The Truth About the Invisible Empire, Knights of the Ku Klux Klan. Portland, Ore.: Pacific Northwest Domain, 1922.

E155 Saxon, William A. Knight Vale of the K. K. K. Columbus, Ohio: Patriot Publishing Company, 1924.

A fictional account of the Klan's opposition to "the menace of Papal autocracy."

E156 Schactman, Max. The Ziegler Frame-Up. Chicago: International Labor Defense, 1925.

E157 Shannon, David A. Between the Wars: America, 1919-1941. Boston: Houghton Mifflin Company, 1965.

A brief discussion of the Klan's rise to prominence during the 1920s.

E158 _____. Twentieth Century America: The United States Since the 1890's. Vol. II: The Twenties and Thirties. 4th ed. Chicago: Rand McNally & Company, 1977.

This volume contains references to the KKK's "revival" and some of its activities, including the Stephenson affair in Indiana.

E159 Shay, Frank. Judge Lynch; His First Hundred Years. New York: Washburn, 1938.

The KKK's strength is exemplified by the situation in Tampa, Florida, where the Klan controlled most of the appointments to municipal positions and could prevent Klan members from being convicted of criminal acts.

E160   Siegfried, Andre. America Comes of Age: A French
       Analysis. New York: Harcourt, Brace and Com-
       pany, 1927.

       Impressions of the KKK; its origins, leaders,
       principles, appeal to various groups in different
       parts of the country, and its weaknesses are pre-
       sented by a French scholar.

E161   Simkins, Francis B., and Charles P. Roland. A
       History of the South. 4th ed. New York: Alfred
       A. Knopf, 1972.

       (See B98.)

E162   Simmons, William J. America's Menace, or The
       Enemy Within. Atlanta: Bureau of Patriotic Books,
       1926.

       Imperial Wizard William Simmons presents his
       views on the "alien element," which he sees as
       America's menace, and his solution to the problem
       being the "100% Protestant Americanism" of the
       KKK. Simmons also comments on the power strug-
       gle within the Klan between himself and his suc-
       cessor, Hiram Evans.

E163   _____. Article in Reply to Charges Made Against
       the Ku Klux Klan. n. p., 192?.

       The first attempt on the part of the Imperial Wiz-
       ard to counter the charges made against the Klan
       by the New York World, by stating the principles
       and goals of the KKK.

E164   _____. Imperial Proclamation of the Imperial
       Wizard, Emperor of the Invisible Empire, Knights
       of the Ku Klux Klan. Atlanta: Knights of the Ku
       Klux Klan, 1917.

E165   _____. The Klan Unmasked. Atlanta: Wm. E.
       Thompson Publishing Co., 1923.

       The founder of the "revived" KKK presents one of
       the first "official" statements of the Klan's pur-
       poses, principles, and goals--claiming to be the
       friend of all (regardless of race, religion, or color),

yet defending the idea that only white Protestants
should govern the country.

E166   _____. The Ku Klux Klan: Yesterday, Today and
Forever. Atlanta: Ku Klux Klan Press, 1916.

The first Imperial Wizard of the "revised" Ku Klux
Klan discusses how the new Klan came about and
states the principles of that organization.

E167   _____. Minutes of the Imperial Kloncilium, Knights
of the Ku Klux Klan; Meeting of May 1 and 2, 1923,
which ratified W. J. Simmons' Agreement with the
Knights of the Ku Klux Klan, Together with Certi-
fied Copies of All Litigation Instituted by W. J.
Simmons Against the Imperial Wizard and the
Knights of the Ku Klux Klan. Atlanta: n. p. , 1923.

E168   Sims, Patsy. The Klan. New York: Stein & Day,
1978.

An examination of the membership, power, and
status of the KKK in the contemporary South. Much
of the information presented was gathered from interviews with local Klan leaders.

E169   _____. The Klan Shall Rise Again. New York:
Stein & Day, 1977.

E170   Skaggs, William H. The Southern Oligarchy. New
York: Devin-Adair Company, 1924.

(See B101.)

E171   Snyder, Louis L. , and Richard Morris, eds. A
Treasury of Great Reporting. New York: Simon
& Schuster, 1949.

Excerpts from the New York World's exposé of
the Ku Klux Klan are included.

E172   Stanton, E. F. 'Christ and Other Klansmen'; or
'Lives of Love'; the Cream of the Bible Spread
upon Klanism. Kansas City, Mo. : Stanton &
Harper, 1924.

E173   Steen, Ralph W. Twentieth Century Texas; An Eco-

nomic and Social History.   Austin: Steck Company,
Publishers,   1942.

E174   Stroud,   Malden (Mrs.).   Poems and Other Matter on
the Ku Klux Klan.   Hammond,   Ind. :   Printed for
the Protestant Non-Klan Society,   1925.

The intolerance and bigotry of the Klan is depicted
"poetically" in this volume.

E175   Synnestvedt,   Sig.   The White Response to Black Eman-
cipation; Second-Class Citizenship in the United
States Since Reconstruction.   New York: Macmillan Company,   1972.

(See B105.)

E176   Tenenbaum,   Samuel.   Why Men Hate.   New York:
Beechhurst Press,   1947.

A brief profile of the KKK,   calling the Klan an organization that "sold hate and mistrust. "   Information is also provided about the financial dealings
of Klan leaders Simmons and Evans and about some
of the activities of the Klan.

E177   Tindall,   George B.   The Emergence of the New South,
1913-1945.   Vol.   X of A History of the South.
Edited by Wendell H.   Stephenson and E.   Merton
Coulter.   10 vols.   Baton Rouge: Louisiana State
University Press,   1967.

A general discussion of the organization and leadership of the "revived" Klan is included.

E178   The Truth About the Notre Dame Riot on Saturday May
17th,   1924.   Indianapolis: Fiery Cross Publishing
Co. ,   1924.

E179   Tucker,   Howard A.   A History of Governor Walton's
War on Ku Klux Klan; The Invisible Empire.   Oklahoma City: Southwest Publishing Company,   1923.

A profile of Governor John Walton and the events
in Oklahoma that led to his declaration of martial
law in the Tulsa area as a result of an outbreak of
KKK terrorism and violence.

E180   Turnbull, George S. An Oregon Crusader. Portland,
        Ore.: Binfords & Mort, Publishers, 1955.

> An account of Oregon newspaperman George Put-
> nam and his editorial campaign against the Klan, as
> the "Invisible Empire" tried to unseat Ben Olcott
> from the governorship and make it illegal for
> parochial schools to operate in Oregon. Despite
> attempts to boycott his paper and put him out of
> business, Putnam continued his journalistic attacks
> on the KKK throughout the election campaign and
> beyond.

E181   Turner, William W. Power on the Right. Berkeley,
        Calif.: Ramparts Press, 1971.

> A discussion of the leadership and activities of the
> post-World War II KKK.

E182   Uchill, Ida L. Pioneers, Peddlers, and Tsadikim.
        Denver: Sage Books, 1957.

> A very brief description of the response of the
> Jewish community in Colorado to the Klan's pres-
> ence in that state during the 1920s.

E183   Vander Zanden, James W. Race Relations in Transi-
        tion; The Segregation Crisis in the South. New
        York: Random House, 1965.

> A sociological analysis of the Klan of the mid-1950s;
> the people who join the KKK and why.

E184   Watters, Pat. Down to Now; Reflections on the South-
        ern Civil Rights Movement. New York: Pantheon
        Books, 1971.

> A brief report on KKK activities during the desegre-
> gation drive in St. Augustine, Florida.

E185   White, Bishop Alma. Heroes of the Fiery Cross.
        Zarephath, N.J.: Good Citizen, 1928.

> The KKK is depicted as the defender of "Ameri-
> canism" in its opposition to immigration, Catholics,
> Jews, Reds, Immorality, and Al Smith, and in its
> support of white supremacy and the teaching of the
> Bible in public schools.

E186   _____. Klansmen: Guardians of Liberty. Zare-
            phath, N. J. : Good Citizen, 1926.

            This volume attempts to show the reader "the de-
            sire of the Roman Catholic hierarchy to control the
            minds of men and to take from them their own de-
            sire of liberty and freedom" and why the KKK justly
            deserves to be called the "Guardians of Liberty, "
            while the Catholic Church should be referred to as
            the "Assassins of Liberty. "

E187   _____. The Ku Klux Klan in Prophecy. Zarephath,
            N. J. : Good Citizen, 1925.

            This tract attempts to find Biblical justification for
            the KKK, especially in its opposition to Roman
            Catholicism.

E188   Whitehead, Don. Attack on Terror; The FBI Against
            the Ku Klux Klan in Mississippi. New York: Funk
            & Wagnalls, 1970.

            The story of the FBI's investigation into the deaths
            of three civil-rights workers in Mississippi and
            the eventual arrest and trial of Klan members for
            those murders.

E189   Wilhoit, Francis M. The Politics of Massive Re-
            sistance. New York: George Braziller, 1973.

            A discussion of the KKK since the Supreme Court's
            school-integration decision, and its efforts to pre-
            vent the implementation of desegregation orders.

E190   Williams, Robert F. Negroes with Guns. New York:
            Marzani & Munsell, 1962.

            The account of some black activists in North Caro-
            lina, who responded to KKK violence by firing back
            at the Klan, as told by the leader of that black
            group.

E191   Winter, Paul M. What Price Tolerance. Hewlett,
            N. Y. : All-American Book, Lecture and Research
            Bureau, 1928.

            The KKK is here viewed in a positive light as the

author attempts to apologize for some of the excesses of the Klan, while extolling its position on
the virtues of "100% Americanism" (in this case
anti-Catholicism). A discussion of actions against
"peaceful" KKK demonstrations, which contains
photos of the 1927 KKK riot in New York, is also
included.

E192 Witcher, Walter C. The Reign of Terror in Oklahoma;
A Detailed Account of the Klan's Barbarous Practices and Brutal Outrages Against Individuals; Its
Control Over Judges and Juries and Governor Walton's Heroic Fight, Including a General Exposure
of Klan Secrets, Sham and Hypocrisy.   Fort Worth,
Texas: W. C. Witcher, 1923.

E193 _____. The Unveiling of the Ku Klux Klan; Being
a Concise and Condensed Analysis of the Philosophy
of the Ku Klux Klan Together with an Exposure of
Its Intrigues, Conspiracies, and Sham Patriotism.
Fort Worth, Texas: American Constitution League,
1922.

E194 Women of the Ku Klux Klan. Constitution and Laws of
the Women of the Ku Klux Klan. Adopted by First
Imperial Klonvocation at St. Louis, Missouri, on
the Sixth Day of January, 1927. Little Rock, Ark.:
n. p., 1927.

E195 _____. Installation Ceremonies.   n. p., n. d.

E196 _____. Kloran, or Ritual of the Women of the Ku
Klux Klan. Little Rock, Ark.: n. p., 192?.

The female unit of the KKK outlines its own principles, rituals, and ceremonies in these three documents.

E197 Wright, Walter C. Religious and Patriotic Ideals of
the Ku Klux Klan; Being a Plain, Practical and
Thorough Exposition of the Principles, Purposes
and Practices of the Ku Klux Klan; A Textbook on
Klan Kraft for the Instruction of Klansmen and the
Information of Non-Klansmen. Waco, Texas:
Grove Printing Company, 1926.

SECTION F: ARTICLES

F1   Abbey, Sue W. "The Ku Klux Klan in Arizona, 1921-
      1925." Journal of Arizona History, XIV (Spring,
      1973), 10-30.

      A study of KKK organization and activity in Arizona,
      where it attempted an unsuccessful entry into the
      political arena.

F2   Ackerman, Curtis. "K K Knavery." New Times, IV
      (May 30, 1975), 41.

      A report on a Klan rally held in Pennsylvania.

F3   "AFL-CIO Fights Klan Infiltration: Grand Dragon's
      Claim of 25, 000 Unionists Under the Robes Draws
      Heated Denials, but Federation Sees Serious Problem
      If Rank and File in South Threaten National Policy."
      Business Week, (October 23, 1965), 47-48.

      Reports of increasing Klan membership among the
      ranks of southern union members and responses to
      this claim by southern labor leaders.

F4   "Again, the Klan." Time, XLV (May 20, 1946), 20.

      The Klan announces its post-World War II revival in
      ceremonies held at Stone Mountain, Georgia.

F5   Aikman, Duncan. "Prairie Fire." American Mercury,
      VI (October, 1925), 209-14.

      A look at the development and the appeal of the KKK.

F6   "Alabama Aroused." Outlook, CXLVII (November 2,
      1927), 261.

      The Attorney-General of Alabama renounces his KKK

membership and vows to bring Klan law-breakers to justice.

F7 "Alabama's Floggers." Literary Digest, XCV (October 29, 1927), 11-12.

Klan members are indicted by a grand jury for recent floggings in Alabama.

F8 Alexander, Charles C. "Defeat, Decline, Disintegration: The Ku Klux Klan in Arkansas, 1924 and After." Arkansas Historical Quarterly, XXII (Winter, 1963), 311-31.

The KKK meets with some success in the political arena in Arkansas, but eventually loses its influence as its major candidates are defeated and the national Democratic party nominates Al Smith for President.

F9 _____. "Kleagles and Cash: The Ku Klux Klan as a Business Organization, 1919-1930." Business History Review, XXXIX (Autumn, 1965), 348-67.

An analysis and discussion of the Klan's financial activities during the '20s. The view of the KKK as a business venture is seen by the author as one reason for its eventual failure.

F10 _____. "Secrecy Bids for Power: The Ku Klux Klan in Texas Politics in the 1920's." Mid-America, XLVI (January, 1964), 3-28.

A discussion of how the KKK got started in Texas, including the rise to prominence of Hiram W. Evans and the Klan's political activities until it was defeated by Miriam Ferguson.

F11 _____. "White-Robed Reformers: The Ku Klux Klan Comes to Arkansas." Arkansas Historical Quarterly, XXII (Spring, 1963), 8-23.

A discussion of the KKK, its appeal to fundamentalist attitudes in Arkansas, and its activities in defense of these ideals.

F12 _____. "White Robes in Politics: The Ku Klux Klan in Arkansas, 1922-1924." Arkansas Historical Quarterly, XXII (Autumn, 1963), 195-214.

The KKK challenges the regular Democratic party in Arkansas by supporting its own candidates in local elections and the Republican Presidential nominee in the 1924 election.

F13   Allen, Devere. "Substitutes for Brotherhood." World Tomorrow, VII (March, 1924), 74-76.

The KKK is viewed as another of the many "societies" enlisting members; however, while it is pointed out that these other groups also have some restrictions in their membership, the Klan does little to eliminate prejudice and intolerance in this country.

F14   Allen, Fredrick L. "K K K." Literary Digest, CXXIV (October 9, 1937), 15-17.

(See C2.)

F15   Allen, Lee N. "The Democratic Presidential Primary Election of 1924 in Texas." Southwestern Historical Quarterly, LXI (April, 1958), 474-93.

A discussion of the Klan's role in Presidential politics in Texas.

F16   _____. "The McAdoo Campaign for the Presidential Nomination in 1924." Journal of Southern History, XXIX (May, 1963), 211-28.

An analysis of William McAdoo's position on the KKK during the campaign for the Democratic Presidential nomination in 1924 and how that position may have lost the nomination for McAdoo.

F17   "Alma Mater, K. K. K. " New Republic, XXXVI (September 5, 1923), 35-36.

A scenario of what Valparaiso University would be like if it was sold to the KKK.

F18   Alsop, Stewart. "Portrait of a Klansman." Saturday Evening Post, CCXXXIX (April 9, 1966), 23-27.

A profile of a local KKK leader in North Carolina.

F19   "And These Are the Children of God. " Collier's National Weekly, CXXIV (August 6, 1949), 74.

Editorial comment on the indoctrination of small children into the Ku Klux Klan.

F20 "Anti-Racists Mobilize in Louisville." Southern Patriot, XXXIII (September, 1975), 8.

The Klan is selected as a target of a school-desegregation rally in Louisville, Kentucky.

F21 Apker, B. M. "The Ku Klux Klan Menace." Notre Dame Lawyer, XXIII (May, 1948), 556-61.

Legal maneuvers to control KKK activities are discussed in light of reported increases in Klan membership.

F22 Arisman, J. Michael. "Gathering of the Klan." Commonweal, LXXXII (June 11, 1965), 373-74.

Reflections on an uneventful Klan march in Durham, North Carolina.

F23 Arnall, Ellis. "My Battle Against the Klan." Coronet, XX (October, 1946), 3-8.

The governor of Georgia recounts some of the recent KKK activities in that state, and his attempts to halt the Klan.

F24 "Arnall Moves to Dissolve Klan." Christian Century, LXIII (July 3, 1946), 829.

The governor of Georgia seeks to disband the KKK by having the courts revoke its charter.

F25 Atwater, Richard. "Grand Jury Indicts Klan." Space City, III (June 15, 1971), 7.

A Houston grand jury indicts several Klan members for a recent wave of bombings and terrorism against leftist and liberal groups.

F26 Babich, Y. "Ku Klux Klan as an Instrument of Reactionary Forces." International Affairs, (October, 1968), 99-104.

A discussion of the KKK as a proponent of ideological

racism and the methods used by the Klan to further that ideology.

F27 "Backfire." Time, LVI (September 11, 1950), 26-27.

A Klan raid on a Negro nightclub in South Carolina leaves a KKK member of the police force dead.

F28 "Bad Medicine for the Klan." Life, XLIV (January 27, 1958), 26-28.

A band of North Carolina Indians break up a Klan rally.

F29 Bagnall, Robert W. "The Spirit of the Ku Klux Klan." Opportunity, I (September, 1923), 265-67.

A discussion of the KKK and its guiding ideology, an ideology that is held by more than just Klan members.

F30 Baker, Bryan. "Klan Bust!" Space City, II (June 1, 1971), 6.

A report that KKK members in Houston were arrested for possessing materials for making bombs.

F31 "Baltimore Bookman Fight Against KKK Terrorism." Publishers Weekly, CXCI (March 27, 1967), 35-36.

The Klan acts against a Baltimore bookstore owner for selling "communist literature."

F32 Barrett, George. "Montgomery: Testing Ground." New York Times Magazine, (December 16, 1956), 8-9+.

The KKK tries to prevent Montgomery, Alabama, Negroes led by Martin Luther King, Jr., from desegregating the city's buses.

F33 Barron, John. "The FBI's Secret War Against the Ku Klux Klan." Reader's Digest, LXXXVIII (January, 1966), 87-92.

Incidents of FBI action against the KKK are cited as an answer to criticism that the FBI has done little to halt Klan activities.

F34   Beazell, W. P.   "The Rise of the Ku Klux Klan."
       World Tomorrow, VII (March, 1924), 71-73.

       The author sees the "revived" Klan as having gone
       through three periods: 1) the "legendary," under
       the influence of William Simmons, who got the idea
       for a revival of the KKK; 2) the "commercial," un-
       der the influence of Edward Clarke, who turned the
       Klan into a profit-making operation; and 3) the "po-
       litical," under the influence of Hiram Evans, who
       hoped to gain usable political power for the KKK.

F35   Beirman, Irving. "Alabama Rips Off the Hood."
       Christian Science Monitor Magazine Section, (July
       2, 1949), 3.

       A report on the passage of a bill in Alabama that
       outlaws the wearing of masks, such as those worn
       by the Ku Klux Klan.

F36   Bell, Edward P.   "Israel Zangwill on the Ku Klux
       Klan." Landmark, VI (June, 1924), 411-18.

       Israel Zangwill responds to remarks by Imperial
       Wizard Evans concerning the "Nordic myth" with
       examples of the "Americanism" of Jews, Catholics,
       and Negroes.

F37   Bentley, Max.   "The Ku Klux Klan in Indiana." Mc-
       Clure's, LVII (May, 1924), 23-33.

       A positive look at the KKK in Indiana, its influence
       on the political scene, and its ability to act as a
       law-enforcement group under the authority of an
       old 19th-century horse-stealing statute.

F38   _____.   "The Ku Klux Klan in Texas." McClure's,
       LVII (May, 1924), 11-21.

       A discussion of the organization and growth of the
       Klan in Texas, and some of the unlawful methods
       the KKK employs to enforce its strict moral stand-
       ards.

F39   _____.   "'Let's Brush Them Aside.'" Collier's
       National Weekly, LXXIV (November 22, 1924), 21.

       The governor of Louisiana, Henry Fuqua, unmasks the KKK and attempts to bring peace to that state.

F40 _____. "A Texan Challenges the Klan." Collier's National Weekly, LXXII (November 3, 1923), 12+.

A look at the rather extensive inroads the KKK has made into the political life of the state of Texas.

F41 Berman, Daniel M. "Hugo L. Black: The Early Years." Catholic University of America Law Review, VIII (May, 1959), 103-16.

A discussion of Supreme Court Justice Hugo Black's life in Alabama and the conditions that led to his membership in the KKK.

F42 Berry, Brewton. "The Myth of the Vanishing Indian." Phylon, XXI (Spring, 1960), 51-57.

The attack and disruption of a KKK rally by the Lumbee Indians of North Carolina is cited as evidence that the Indian has not vanished.

F43 Besal, Dorothy. "'Reasonable' Racism." Community, XXIV (May, 1965), 3.

Imperial Wizard James Venable of the National Association of the Ku Klux Klan (as opposed to Robert Shelton's United Klans of America, Knights of the KKK, Inc.) presents his views of nonviolent racism.

F44 Betten, Neil. "Nativism and the Klan in Town and City: Valparaiso and Gary, Indiana." Studies in History and Society, IV (1973), 3-16.

A look at the Klan's strength and influence in Indiana, and the appeal of the KKK to rural (Valparaiso) and urban (Gary) residents of that state.

F45 "Black: Klan Member on the Supreme Court? New Evidence Comes to Light." Newsweek, X (September 20, 1937), 9-12.

The controversy concerning Hugo Black's membership in the KKK continues.

F46   "Black Marines Battle Ku Klux Klan at Camp Pendleton Base. " Black Scholar, VIII (April, 1977), 46-49.

A report on a recent attack on a Klan meeting at a Marine base, and the results of that skirmish. Also included is a very brief history of the KKK and a list of Klan activities during the 1970s.

F47   Blake, Aldrich. "Oklahoma's Klan-Fighting Governor. " Nation, CXVII (October 3, 1923), 353.

A profile of Governor John Walton and his attempts to stop KKK lawlessness in Oklahoma.

F48   Bliss, David. "Antiwar Movement Attacks Links of Houston Police to Ku Klux Klan. " Militant, XXXIV (November 27, 1970), 3.

A report on efforts of activist groups in the Houston area to publicize a connection between the Houston police and the local KKK organization.

F49   Bliven, Bruce. "From the Oklahoma Front. " New Republic, XXXVI (October 17, 1923), 202-05.

A report on the political battle in Oklahoma between Governor John Walton and the KKK.

F50   "'Bloody Herrin' Again. " Literary Digest, LXXXII (September 13, 1924), 9.

A look at the situation in the southern Illinois mining town of Herrin, where KKK forces were involved in open "warfare" against state and local authorities.

F51   Bohn, Frank. "The Ku Klux Klan Interpreted. " American Journal of Sociology, XXX (January, 1925), 385-407.

An analysis of the Klan as it existed in Ohio during the 1920s. Imperial Wizard William Simmons's philosophy and rituals are seen as appealing to the disillusioned society.

F52   Boyd, Thomas. "Defying the Klan. " Forum, LXXVI (July, 1926), 48-56.

A discussion of Georgia newsman Julian Harris and his editorial campaign against the Klan.

F53   Braxton, Lee. "They Spoke Out for Decency." Rotarian, LXXXIII (September, 1953), 29+.

A report on two North Carolina newspapermen who won the Pulitzer Prize for their editorial efforts against the KKK.

F54   Brier, Royce. "Nightshirt Knights." Forum, CVI (July, 1946), 54-55.

A condemnation of the current KKK: what it represents and its recent activities.

F55   "Broken Monopoly." Time, LV (March 20, 1950), 20.

Two juries find Klan members guilty of various acts against Negroes in Georgia and South Carolina.

F56   Broun, Heywood. "Up Pops the Wizard." New Republic, XCIX (July 21, 1939), 186-87.

A report on the new Imperial Wizard of the Ku Klux Klan, James A. Colescott.

F57   Brownell, Blaine A. "Birmingham, Alabama: New South City in the 1920's." Journal of Southern History, XXXVIII (February, 1972), 21-48.

A description of KKK growth and political influence in this southern city.

F58   Brundidge, Harry T. "The Klan Rides Again." Cosmopolitan, CXXI (August, 1946), 27.

F59   Buckner, George W., Jr. "Probe a Rebirth of Hoosier Klan." Christian Century, LXIII (November 27, 1946), 1446.

A report that the KKK is beginning to reorganize itself in Indiana.

F60   Budenz, Louis F. "There's Mud on Indiana's White Robes." Nation, CXXV (July 27, 1927), 81-82.

Klan activities continue in Indiana after the imprisonment of KKK leader David Stephenson.

F61   Burbank, Garin. "Agrarian Radicals and Their Oppo-
       nents: Political Conflict in Southern Oklahoma, 1910-
       1924. " Journal of American History, LVIII (1971),
       5-23.

       An analysis of the political battle in Oklahoma be-
       tween the Klan and the Farm-Labor Union.

F62   Burner, David B. "The Democratic Party in the Elec-
       tion of 1924. " Mid-America, XLVI (1964), 92-113.

       A discussion of the leading Democratic Presidential
       Candidates in 1924, their position on the KKK, how
       that stand affected their candidacy, and the Klan is-
       sue dispute at the national convention.

F63   ". . . But the Klan. " America, CX (May 9, 1964), 619-
       20.

       A report of an increase in Klan activities and the
       efforts of a New Orleans reporter to expose the
       Klan's activities.

F64   "Button-Down Bed Sheets. " Newsweek, LXII (August
       26, 1963), 32-33.

       The KKK adopts some of the nonviolent tactics of
       Martin Luther King, Jr. , as it tries to gain respec-
       tability both inside and outside the South.

F65   Byrne, Kevin, and Oliver Houghton. "Texas Klan Ral-
       ly; Cow Pasture Politics. " Space City, III (August
       31, 1971), 15.

       A report of a KKK rally outside of Houston at which
       Imperial Wizard Robert Shelton spoke.

F66   Calderwood, William. "The Decline of the Progressive
       Party in Saskatchewan, 1925-1930. " Saskatchewan
       History, XXI (Autumn, 1968), 81-99.

       An analysis of the Klan's role in the politics of Sas-
       katchewan, as the Progressives and Conservatives
       tried to gain power from the current Liberal govern-
       ment.

F67   _____ . "Religious Reactions to the Ku Klux Klan in
       Saskatchewan. " Saskatchewan History, XXVI (Au-
       tumn, 1973), 103-14.

       A study of the KKK's appeal as a religious organiza-
       tion, and the success this approach had in Saskatch-
       ewan. A look at Protestant reaction, both for and
       against the Klan, and Catholic and Jewish reactions
       against the Klan is also included.

F68   Callaway, E. E. "Notes on a Kleage. " American
       Mercury, XLIII (February, 1938), 248-49.

       A letter from a reader who feels that the Klan has
       helped reduce prejudice in the South (by setting a
       bad example), and that Supreme Court Justice Hugo
       Black is not a KKK member.

F69   Campbell, W. D. "World of the Redneck. " Katallagete,
       V (Spring, 1974), 34-40. (Reprinted in Christianity
       and Crisis, XXXIV [May 27, 1974], 111-18.)

F69a   "Can the Ku Klux Klan Survive in Oklahoma?" Harlow's
       Weekly, XXIII (September 6, 1924), 6-7.

       The KKK's survival in Oklahoma is questioned due
       to internal disagreements among Klan members.

F70   "Canada's 'Keep-Out' to Klanism. " Literary Digest,
       LXXVI (February 3, 1923), 20-21.

       A report on efforts in Canada to prevent the spread
       of the KKK across its borders.

F71   Carrott, M. B. "The Supreme Court and Minority
       Rights in the Nineteen-Twenties. " Northwest Ohio
       Quarterly, XLI (1969), 144-56.

       A study of Supreme Court decisions that dealt with
       minority rights, including its overturning of the KKK-
       inspired Oregon law banning parochial schools and
       other decisions affecting the Klan.

F72   "Carter and the KKK. " New Republic, CXXXVI (Febru-
       ary 4, 1957), 6.

       An incident in Alabama brings forth the link between
       the KKK and the White Citizens Councils.

F73   "Casting Out the Klan. "   Independent, CXIII (September 13, 1924), 141.

Editorial comment on statements by Presidential candidates Dawes and LaFollette opposing the KKK and urging President Coolidge to do the same.

F74   Catchpole, Terry. "Operation Contempt. " National Review, XVIII (February 22, 1966), 152.

A report on the second round of hearings in the House Un-American Activities Committee's investigation of the KKK and some of the witnesses called to testify.

F75   Catt, Carrie. "Three Super States. " Woman Citizen, IX (October 18, 1924), 10-11+.

A discussion of the Klan's anti-Catholic principles, including Papal domination and public education.

F76   Chalk, David. "Klanswomen; In the New South the Ku Klux Klan Is Very Much a Family Affair. " New Dawn, I (September, 1976), 37-41.

A pictorial essay on female Klan members in Louisiana.

F77   Chalmers, David. "The Ku Klux Klan in Politics in the 1920's. " Mississippi Quarterly, XVIII (Fall, 1965), 234-47.

A discussion of the KKK's strength and influence in the political arena on both the national and state levels.

F78   _____. "The Ku Klux Klan in the Sunshine State: The 1920's. " Florida Historical Quarterly, XLII (January, 1964), 209-15.

A study of the KKK's activities in Florida on the political scene and in other areas.

F79   Chinn, Richard. "April 24/Here, There & Everywhere. " Win, VII (June, 1971), 14.

The KKK marches in Indiana to protest against antiwar demonstrations held in Washington and across the country.

F80 Clark, Malcolm, Jr. "The Bigot Disclosed: 90 Years of Nativism. " Oregon Historical Quarterly, LXXV (June, 1974), 108-90.

An analysis of the KKK in Oregon and how the Klan came to control so much political influence in that state.

F81 "The Clash in the Klan. " Literary Digest, LXXVII (April 21, 1923), 13.

Former Imperial Wizard William Simmons attempts to establish a Klan group for women and runs into opposition from current Imperial Wizard Hiram Evans.

F82 Cleghorn, Reese. "Kommemorating an Anniversary (but very quietly). " Atlanta Magazine, V (November, 1965), 30-34+.

A survey of the history and activities of the KKK, especially in Georgia, on the occasion of the 50th anniversary of the Klan's "revival" (1915-65).

F83 Cline, Leonard L. "In Darkest Louisiana. " Nation, CXVI (March 14, 1923), 292-93.

A discussion of the situation in the Mer Rouge, Louisiana, area that led to the murder of two men by the KKK.

F84 Coben, Stanley. "The Assault on Victorianism in the Twentieth Century. " American Quarterly, XXVII (December, 1975), 604-25.

The Klan is seen as trying to keep Victorian culture alive in America. Some of the various methods used to combat the Klan are also mentioned.

F85 Cole, Nancy. "How FBI Aided Klan Terrorists. " Militant, XXXIX (December 12, 1975), 3.

A former FBI informer implies that the FBI allowed the KKK to carry out some of its activities against civil-rights workers in the South.

F86 _____.   "Informer Reveals FBI's Role in Ku Klux Klan Attacks. "   Intercontinental Press, XIII (December 15, 1975), 758-59.

A former FBI informant accuses the FBI of cooperating in KKK activities against the civil-rights movement.

F87 Collings, Anthony.   "Klansman at Large. "   Newsweek, XCI (March 20, 1978), 45.

KKK leader David Duke becomes a fugitive from the British police as he recruits new members in England.

F88 Collins, Fredrick L.   "Way Down East with the K. K. K. " Collier's National Weekly, LXXII (December 15, 1923), 12+.

A look at the KKK and its increasing appeal outside the South, especially in the state of Maine.

F89 Colman, Louis.   "The Klan Revives. "   Nation, CXXXIX (July 4, 1934), 20.

A letter to the editor concerning a "revival" of KKK activities against the International Labor Defense, a group helping to defend the Scottsboro boys.

F90 "Colonel Simmons and $146, 000, from K. K. K. to K. F. S. "   Literary Digest, LXXX (March 8, 1924), 36-40.

A report on the internal strife in the KKK that led William Simmons, the man who "revived" the Klan, to withdraw from the organization and contemplate starting a new one.

F91 Commager, Henry S.   "Does the Klan Ride to Its Death?"   Scholastic, XLIX (October 7, 1946), 7.

The lessons of past KKK activities are to be remembered in dealing with the current Klan situation.

F92 "Confirmation from a Strange Source. "   American Federationist, XXIX (December, 1922), 905-06.

While opposing the KKK, the American Federation of

Labor agrees with a recent editorial criticizing the extra-legal activities of Kansas Governor Allen in dealing with the Klan, especially since the same kind of activities were once used against organized labor.

F93   "Congress vs. Extremists." American Legion Magazine, LXXXII (January, 1967), 12-15+.

An interview with the Chairman, Staff Director, and Chief Counsel for the House Un-American Activities Committee concerning its investigation of the Ku Klux Klan and other extremist groups.

F94   Cook, Samuel D.   "Political Movements and Organizations." Journal of Politics, XXVI (February, 1964), 130-53.

A brief observation on the Klan's attempts in the 1960s to regain its influence of the '20s and a description of White Citizens Councils as "country club Klans."

F95   Cowan, W. H.   "HUAC and the Klan." Christianity and Crisis, XXV (May 17, 1965), 103-04.

The House Un-American Activities Committee's upcoming investigation of the Klan is viewed with reservations because of HUAC's tactics.

F96   "Crackdown on the Klan." Time, LIX (February 25, 1952), 28.

The FBI arrests ten Klansmen on kidnapping charges resulting from a KKK "reign of terror" in North Carolina.

F97   Craven, Charles.   "The Robeson County Indian Uprising Against the KKK." South Atlantic Quarterly, LVII (Autumn, 1968), 433-42.

A report on the events that led to a group of North Carolina Indians attacking and disrupting a KKK rally.

F98   "Crosses of Fire." Newsweek, XXVII (April 8, 1946), 21-22.

Klan membership begins to increase as the KKK plans

to "combat" union organizers in the South and keep Negroes from exercising their right to vote.

F99   Crowell, Chester T. "The Collapse of Constitutional Government." Independent, CIX (December 9, 1922), 333-34, and CX (January 6, 1923), 8-9.

A discussion of KKK activities in a recent primary election in Texas and the Klan's anti-Catholic and anti-Jewish policies and how they conflict with constitutional principles.

F100   Crownover, Donald A. "The Ku Klux Klan in Lancaster County: 1923-24." Journal of the Lancaster County Historical Society, LXVIII (1964), 63-77.

A study of the organization and activities of the KKK in Lancaster County, Pennsylvania.

F101   Cushman, Terry, and Kay Stacy. "Klan in Twenties; Terror Group Reborn." Worker's Power, No. 31 (October 17, 1975), 3.

A brief description of the KKK and its activities in the years following World War I.

F102   _____. "The Klan's New Face; Planning for Genocide." Worker's Power, No. 32 (October 24, 1975), 8.

A look at the KKK's activities in opposition to the recent civil-rights movement.

F103   _____. "Klan's Record--100 Years of Terror." Worker's Power, No. 30 (October 2, 1975), 15.

A brief overview of the KKK's activities in the United States.

F104   Daniels, Jonathan. "K. K. K. Versus U. S. O. " Nation, CLIII (November 8, 1941), 456.

The KKK opposes Catholic and Jewish participation in the USO.

F105   "Dark Days in Weird Week." Time, LXXXVI (October 29, 1965), 29.

A report on the KKK investigation by the House Un-American Activities Committee.

F106   Davis, James H.   "Colorado Under the Klan." <u>Colorado Magazine</u>, XLII (Spring, 1965), 83-108.

Clarence Morley, the KKK-supported governor of Colorado runs into opposition in his attempts to place the state government in control of the Klan.

F107   "Day of Accusation in Mississippi." <u>Life</u>, LVII (December 18, 1964), 34-37.

Klansmen charged with the murders of civil-rights workers Goodman, Schwerner, and Chaney are arraigned and then released.

F108   Deaton, Ron.   "Klan Revival; Work of D. Duke." <u>Progressive</u>, XXXIX (June, 1975), 29.

A brief analysis of the image and appeal of the young KKK leader David Duke.

F109   "A Defense of the Ku Klux Klan." <u>Literary Digest</u>, LXXVI (January 20, 1923), 18-19.

A survey of recent newspaper articles and editorials defending the Klan against various charges.

F110   Degler, Carl N.   "A Century of the Klans: A Review Article." <u>Journal of Southern History</u>, XXXI (November, 1965), 435-43.

While basically a review article of the Alexander (see E2), Chalmers (E29), and Randel (E144) books, the author provides some of his own analysis and insight into the history of the Ku Klux Klan.

F111   "Democracy or Invisible Empire?" <u>Current Opinion</u>, LXXV (November, 1923), 521-23.

Editorial opinion against the KKK in the wake of its recent victory over Governor Walton of Oklahoma.

F112   DeSilver, Albert.   "Ku Klux Klan--'Soul of Chivalry.'" <u>Nation</u>, CXIII (September 14, 1921), 285-86.

A discussion of William Simmons's reorganization of the KKK and reports of Klan floggings, beatings, and other activities.

F113   Desmond, Shaw.   "K. K. K. :   The Strongest Secret Society on Earth. "   Wide World Magazine, XLVII
(August, 1921), 339-47.

F114   Desmonde, William H.   "The Ku Klux Klan: Some
Psychoanalytic Interpretations. "   Journal of the
Hillside Hospital, III (1954), 219-55.

F115   Devine, Edward T.   "The Klan in Texas. "   Survey,
XLVIII (April 1, 1922), 10-11.

A survey of the attitudes toward the Klan of the people of Texas.

F116   _____.   "More About the Klan. "   Survey, XLVIII
(April 8, 1922), 42-43.

A further report about the Klan's activities in Texas and Texans' attitudes toward the KKK.

F117   Dillon, Marton L.   "Captain Jason W. James, Frontier
Anti-Democrat. "   New Mexico Historical Review,
XXXI (April, 1956), 89-101.

(See C11.)

F118   "Disrobing the KKK. "   New Republic, CXXVI (May
26, 1952), 6.

Klan members are successfully brought to trial for kidnapping in North Carolina.

F119   "Divisible Invisible Empire. "   Newsweek, XXXII (July
19, 1948), 20.

The Georgia Klan splits, as a splinter group or-
ganizes in hopes that it will become a profitable venture.

F120   Douglas, Lloyd C.   "The Patriotism of Hatred. "
Christian Century, XL (October 25, 1923), 1371-
74.

An analysis of the Klan's principles and how it feels about certain minority groups.

F121 Douglas, W. A. S. "Ku Klux." _American Mercury_, XIII (March, 1928), 272-79.

An account of some of the KKK's activities in Oklahoma, including the shooting of a foreign-born oil driller.

F122 "The Drive to Expose Secrets of the Klan. " _U. S. News & World Report_, LVIII (April 12, 1965), 69.

A report on the House Un-American Activities Committee's decision to investigate the KKK and other anti-Klan activities of the federal government.

F123 DuBois, W. E. Burghardt. "The Shape of Fear. " _North American Review_, CCXXIII (June, 1926), 291-304.

A discussion of the methods employed by the Klan to accomplish its goals; the murders at Mer Rouge, Louisiana, are cited as an example.

F124 Duffus, Robert L. "Ancestry and End of the Ku Klux Klan. " _World's Work_, XLVI (September, 1923), 527-36.

Historical comparisons are drawn between the KKK and previous organizations with similar ideals, resulting in a predicted decline of the Klan.

F125 _____. "Counter-mining the Ku Klux Klan. " _World's Work_, XLVI (July, 1923), 275-84.

A report on the work of the Commission on Inter-Racial Cooperation, a southern group trying to combat the effects of the KKK.

F126 _____. "How the Ku Klux Klan Sells Hate. " _World's Work_, XLVI (June, 1923), 174-83.

A discussion of KKK methods, using the murder of two men in Mer Rouge, Louisiana, as an example.

F127 _____. "The Ku Klux Klan in the Middle West. " _World's Work_, XLVI (August, 1923), 363-72.

A discussion of KKK activity, especially in the political arena, in the Midwest. The situation in Kansas is highlighted.

F128 _____. "Saleman of Hate: The Ku Klux Klan." World's Work, XLVI (May, 1923), 31-38.

A discussion of the "revived" KKK, how it was started, and the people who made it a national organization.

F129 Dunbar, Anthony. "Conspiracy on Conspiracy." Katallagete, III (Winter, 1971), 33-38.

A female KKK member is killed and another Klansman is wounded as they attempt to bomb the house of a Jewish businessman in Meridian, Mississippi.

F130 Dunning, Fredrick A. "Ku Klux Fulfills the Scripture." Christian Century, XLI (September 18, 1924), 1205-07.

An analysis of certain passages from the Bible is made; however, no justification can be found for the idea that the Ku Klux Klan was prophesied in the Bible.

F131 "Dying Klansman 'Confesses' to Bombing." Black Panther, XI (March 16, 1974), 5.

A KKK member makes a deathbed confession to the bombing of school buses in Pontiac, Michigan.

F132 Dykeman, Wilma, and James Stokely. "The Klan Tries a Comeback; In the Wake of Desegregation." Commentary, XXIX (January, 1960), 45-51.

A report on Klan activities throughout the South to gain members and exert its influence in the fight against school desegregation.

F133 Early, Tracy. "Klan Kludd: To Be or Not to Be." Christian Century, LXXXIV (February 22, 1967), 236.

A report on recent KKK activities in Virginia, and a comparison of Klan tactics between the 1920s and '60s.

F134   Edmonds, Henry M. "Ignorance Is Power: The Klan. "
       Plain Talk, II (1928), 153-59.

       A southern minister comments on the Klan's use of
       old prejudices to make money for KKK leaders, and
       predicts that the Klan will not last.

F135   Edmonson, Ben G. "Pat Harrison and Mississippi in
       the Presidential Elections of 1924 and 1928. " Jour-
       nal of Mississippi History, XXXIII (November,
       1971), 333-50.

       Democratic Party leaders in Mississippi try to
       maintain party unity in the face of Klan opposition
       to Presidential candidate Al Smith.

F136   "Election Eve in Georgia. " New Republic, CXIX
       (September 6, 1948), 10.

       A report on Klan activities, aimed at keeping
       Negroes from voting in the Georgia primary, to
       ensure a victory for Herman Talmadge.

F137   "End of Hearings on the Klan. " America, CXIV
       (March 12, 1966), 343.

       A report on the progress made by the House Un-
       American Activities Committee in its investigation
       of the Klan.

F138   Evans, Hiram W. "The Ballots Behind the Ku Klux
       Klan. " World's Work, LV (January, 1928), 243-52.

       The Imperial Wizard states the Klan's principles
       and how it plans to further those principles, and
       the Klan's opposition to Al Smith's Presidential
       campaign.

F139   _____. "The Catholic Question as Viewed by the
       Ku Klux Klan. " Current History, XXVI (July,
       1927), 563-68.

       The Imperial Wizard presents the Klan's view of
       Catholics by attempting to show how the doctrines
       and practices of the Catholic Church are not in
       harmony with American principles and institutions.

F140   . "The Klan: Defender of Americanism. "
          Forum, LXXIV (December, 1925), 801-14.

          The Imperial Wizard defends the KKK against earli-
          er comments by William Pattangall (see F405) and
          attempts to put the Klan forth as a patriotic group
          concerned about America.

F141   . "The Klan's Fight for Americanism. "
          North American Review, CCXXIII (March, 1926),
          33-63. (Reprinted in Abrams, Richard M. , and
          Lawrence W. Levine, eds. The Shaping of Twen-
          tieth-Century America: Interpretive Essays. rev.
          2nd ed. Boston: Little, Brown and Company,
          1971; Coben, Stanley, ed. Reform, War and Re-
          action, 1912-1932. New York: Harper & Row,
          Publishers, 1973; Mowry, George E. , ed. The
          Twenties; Fords, Flappers and Fanatics. Engle-
          wood Cliffs, N. J. : Prentice-Hall, 1963; and Tra-
          verso, Edmund, ed. The 1920's; Rhetoric and Re-
          ality. Boston: D. C. Heath and Company, 1964.)

          The KKK's Imperial Wizard presents the Klan's
          principles, which he sums up as a belief in patri-
          otism, the supremacy of the white race, and the
          supremacy of the Protestant religion.

F142 "Even the Klan Has Rights. " Nation, CXV (December
          13, 1922), 654.

          Editorial comment urging some restraint in dealing
          with KKK offenses, in order to avoid breaking the
          law to deal with law-breakers.

F143 Fairlie, Henry. "An Englishman Goes to a Klan
          Meeting. " New York Times Magazine, (May 23,
          1965), 26-27+.

          An English correspondent reflects on a Klan rally
          he witnessed in North Carolina.

F144 Fanning, Jerry, and Bustin, Andy. "KKK Grand
          Dragon Indicted in Houston. " Militant, XXXV (Sep-
          tember 17, 1971), 24.

          A report that a local KKK leader was indicted for

illegal possession of weapons by a Houston grand jury.

F145   "The Fearmongers." Life, LVI (February 7, 1964), 71-78+.

Profiles of the leaders of various extremist groups. Included is Robert Shelton, Imperial Wizard of the KKK.

F146   Feidelson, Charles N. "Alabama's Super Government." Nation, CXXV (September 28, 1927), 311-12.

A report from Alabama that Klan members were found guilty of kidnapping and flogging a young man in a state where the KKK controlled most of the elected officials.

F147   "A Fight for Freedom of the Press." Literary Digest, XC (August 14, 1926), 9.

An Indiana newspaper editor is cited for contempt of court from charges resulting from his editorial campaign against the KKK.

F148   "A Flogging for the Klan." Time, LX (August 11, 1952), 21.

North Carolina Klansmen are arrested and convicted for flogging in an FBI crackdown on the KKK.

F149   Flowers, Richmond. "Southern Plain Talk About the Ku Klux Klan." Look, XXX (May 3, 1966), 36+.

The Attorney-General of Alabama, who conducted an investigation of the KKK, discusses what he learned about the activities and influence of the Klan in Alabama.

F150   Foley, Albert S. "KKK in Mobile, Ala." America, XCVI (December 8, 1956), 298-99.

A report on recent Klan activities in the Mobile area. Activities range from attempted assassination of a Negro political candidate to Sunday church visits.

F151 _____. "New 'Church, ' Old Klan. " America, CXXVII (October 21, 1972), 321-22.

A report on recent Klan activities and intimidations under the guise of the "Assembly of Christian Soldiers, Inc. "

F152 Foltz, C. Roy. "The Ku Klux Klan, a Menace to Society. " American Labor World, (January, 1925), 22-23.

The KKK is cited as an un-American organization because of the Klan's unlawful activities and its exclusion of Catholics, Jews, and aliens, though the author does feel that the original 19th-century KKK served a useful and honorable purpose.

F153 Footlick, Jerrold K. , and Anthony Marro. "G-Men and Klansmen. " Newsweek, LXXXVI (August 25, 1975), 74-75.

Reports of FBI activity against the KKK are released to the public as government officials try to curb the Bureau's intelligence-gathering projects.

F154 "For and Against the Ku Klux Klan. " Literary Digest, LXX (September 24, 1921), 34-40.

A report on the "revived" Klan, its organization, purposes, and membership, and a discussion of recent articles concerning the Klan that appeared in the New York World.

F155 "The Four Klansmen. " Newsweek, LXIV (August 17, 1964), 29.

Four KKK members are arrested for the murder of a Negro Army Reserve officer in Georgia.

F156 Frank, Glenn. "Christianity and Radicalism; Has the Ku Klux Klan the Right to Celebrate Christmas?" Century, CIX (December, 1924), 277-84.

The position is taken that as long as the KKK is opposed to the Christian viewpoint of the brotherhood of humankind, it has no right to carry on its activities in the name of Christianity.

F157   "From the Kreed of Klanishness." World Tomorrow,
       VII (March, 1924), 76-77.

       Excerpts of the KKK's creed, oath, and greeting
       are reprinted from official Klan documents.

F158   Frost, Stanley. "Behind the White Hoods; The Re-
       generation of Oklahoma." Outlook, CXXXV (No-
       vember 21, 1923), 492-95.

       A discussion of the KKK in Oklahoma and its role
       in the impeachment of Governor John Walton.

F159   _____. "Klan, the King, and a Revolution; The
       Regeneration of Oklahoma." Outlook, CXXXV
       (November 28, 1923), 530-31.

       A discussion of the mistakes made by Governor
       John Walton in his handling of the KKK situation
       in Oklahoma, as the war against the Klan continues.

F160   _____. "The Klan Restates Its Case." Outlook,
       CXXXVIII (October 15, 1924), 244-45.

       The KKK attempts to change its image at a nation-
       al Klonvocation in Kansas City, but the principles
       of the Klan remain unchanged.

F161   _____. "The Klan Shows Its Hand in Indiana."
       Outlook, CXXXVII (June 4, 1924), 187-90.

       A report on how the KKK won political control in
       Indiana.

F162   _____. "The Klan's 1/2 of 1 per cent Victory."
       Outlook, CXXXVII (July 9, 1924), 384-87.

       A report on the KKK issue as it arose during the
       1924 Democratic National Convention and how the
       issue was resolved.

F163   _____. "The Masked Politics of the Klan and How
       the Candidacy of Smith May Be Affected." World's
       Work, LV (February, 1928), 399-407.

       A discussion of the Klan's political strength and
       methods, and how it could affect Al Smith's Presi-
       dential campaign.

F164 _____. "Night-Riding Reformers; The Regeneration of Oklahoma." Outlook, CXXV (November 14, 1923), 438-40.

John Walton is impeached as Oklahoma's governor, but the KKK issue continues.

F165 _____. "The Oklahoma Regicides Act." Outlook, CXXXV (November 7, 1923), 395-96.

A report on the impeachment charges being brought against Oklahoma Governor John Walton for his methods used in curbing KKK violence.

F166 _____. "When the Klan Rules." Outlook, CXXXV (December 19, 1923), 674-76; (December 26, 1923), 716-18; CXXXVI (January 2, 1924), 20-24; (January 9, 1924), 64-66; (January 16, 1924), 100-03; (January 23, 1924), 144-47; (January 30, 1924), 183-86; (February 6, 1924), 217-18; (February 13, 1924), 261-64; (February 20, 1924), 308-11; and (February 27, 1924), 350-53.

A series of articles that thoroughly discusses the KKK of the early '20s, from its origins and developments to the people the Klan appeals to, its principles of white supremacy, anti-Catholicism and anti-Semitism, its use of politics to gain influence and power, and the success it has had in politics.

F167 Fry, George T. "The Decline of Bigotry in America." Current History, XXVIII (June, 1928), 396-402.

The Klan's waning influence is seen as evidence that prejudice is declining in the U.S., especially when compared with activities in the colonial and early national periods.

F168 Garson, Robert A. "Political Fundamentalism and Popular Democracy in the 1920's." South Atlantic Quarterly, LXXVI (Spring, 1977), 219-33.

An analysis of the KKK as a group trying to restore order to society in the post-World War I years. Emphasis is on the Klan's efforts to enforce a strict moral code on others.

F169   Gatewood, Willard B. , Jr.   "Politics and Piety in
       North Carolina: The Fundamentalist Crusade at
       High Tide, 1925-1927. " North Carolina Historical
       Review, XLII (July, 1965), 275-90.

       This article contains passing references to KKK ac-
       tivities aimed at defending the fundamentalist ideas
       held by the Klan.

F170   Geyer, Elizabeth.   "The 'New' Ku Klux Klan. "   Crisis,
       LXIII (March, 1956), 139-48.

       A discussion of the activities of the White Citizens
       Councils to prevent court-ordered desegregation
       leads them to be described as a "manicured KKK. "

F171   Goldberg, Robert A.   "The Ku Klux Klan in Madison,
       1922-1927. " Wisconsin Magazine of History, LVIII
       (Autumn, 1974), 31-44.

       A discussion of Klan strength in the Wisconsin
       capital and its activities against immigrant groups
       and trying to police the morals of the community.

F172   Goldenweiser, Alexander.   "Prehistoric K. K. K. 's. "
       World Tomorrow, VII (March, 1924), 81-82.

       A brief look is taken at prior societies whose
       secrecy, costumes, and rituals are similar to
       those of the KKK.   The popularity of the Klan is
       explained by calling the "Invisible Empire" an emo-
       tional safety valve against the dullness of Ameri-
       can society, which does not, however, justify its
       existence.

F173   Good, Paul.   "Klantown, USA. "   Nation, CC (Febru-
       ary 1, 1965), 110-13.

       A report on the situation in Bogalusa, Louisiana,
       which boasts of having the largest KKK concentra-
       tion of any southern town.

F174   Goodman, Walter.   "H. U. A. C. Meets the K. K. K. "
       New York Times Magazine, (December 5, 1965),
       48-49+.

       A report on the investigation of the Ku Klux Klan
       by the House Un-American Activities Committee.

F175 _____. "The Klan Discovers HUAC. " Nation, CCI (November 8, 1965), 328-30.

A report on the Congressional investigation of the Ku Klux Klan being conducted by the House Un-American Activities Committee.

F176 "Grand Dragon Indicted. " Space City, III (September 14, 1971), 5.

A Houston KKK leader is indicted for violation of the Federal Firearms Act.

F177 "Grand Jury Refuses to Indict Klansmen for Killing of Black Man. " Black Panther, VI (May 15, 1971), 5.

A report of a trial in North Carolina in which three Klan members were set free.

F178 "Grand Jury Won't Indict Klansmen. " Space City, II (May 25, 1971), 6.

A news report that three KKK members were freed of murder charges of a black man in North Carolina.

F179 Grant, Jim. "Insurrection in Wilmington. " Southern Patriot, XXIX (March, 1971), 2+.

A report on the situation in Wilmington, North Carolina, where KKK members and Negroes were exchanging gunfire in a clash that began over conditions in local schools.

F180 _____. "Rebellion in Oxford. " Southern Patriot, XXVIII (June, 1970), 1+.

Two Klan members are charged with the murder of a Negro, as violence erupts in a small North Carolina community.

F181 Greene, Ward. "Notes for a History of the Klan. " American Mercury, V (June, 1925), 240-43.

This article presents the thesis that Prohibition was responsible for the rise of the KKK.

F182 Greenway, John. "Country-Western: The Music of

America. " American West, V (November, 1968), 32-41.

Brief mention of the fact that the Klan sponsored many local fiddling competitions during the 1920s.

F183   Gregory, Dick. "And I Ain't Just Whistlin' Dixie. " Ebony, XXVI (August, 1971), 149-50.

A noted black comedian puts the Klan in a humorous, but grim, light.

F184   Griffith, Charles B. , and Donald W. Stewart. "Has a Court of Equity Power to Enjoin Parading by the Ku Klux Klan in Mask?" Central Law Journal, XCVI (November 20, 1923), 384-93.

A discussion of a Kansas court's decision to stop the KKK from parading in their masks.

F185   Grizzard, Vernon. "Fraternity and Brotherhood ... Police and the Klan. " Kudzu, III (September, 1970), 8-9.

A discussion of the similarities in the values held by the police and the Ku Klux Klan.

F186   "Gun-Play and Sudden Death in Herrin. " Literary Digest, LXXXIV (February 21, 1925), 34+.

The story of a "shoot-out" between KKK members and law-enforcement officers in the Illinois mining community of Herrin.

F187   Hapgood, Norman, and Louis Glavis. "The New Thrust of the Ku Klux Klan. " Hearst's International, XLIV (January, 1923), and XLV (April, 1924).

F187a Harlow, Victor E. "The Achievement of the Klan. " Harlow's Weekly, XXIII (July 19, 1924), 1.

Editorial comment about John Walton's election as governor of Oklahoma due to the anti-Klan vote.

F187b _____. "A New Phase in the Klan. " Harlow's Weekly, XXIII (December 6, 1924), 1.

Editorial comment concerning the Klan's program in Oklahoma to remove dissenters from the Oklahoma Klan.

F188   Harris, Abraham I. "The Klan on Trial. " New Republic, XXXV (June 13, 1923), 67-69.

A report of a trial held in Minneapolis in which Klan members were convicted of criminal libel.

F189   Harrison, Morton. "Gentlemen from Indiana. " Atlantic, CXLI (May, 1928), 676-86. (Reprinted in Mowry, George E. , ed. The Twenties; Fords, Flappers and Fanatics. Englewood Cliffs, N. J. : Prentice-Hall, 1963.)

A report on the KKK's growth and control in Indiana due to the efforts of Klan leader David C. Stevenson.

F190   Harsch, Ernie. "Klansmen Arrested in Michigan Bombing. " Militant, XXXV (September 24, 1971), 14.

KKK members are arrested in Pontiac, Michigan, for the bombing of school buses to be used in a busing program to carry out a school-desegregation order.

F191   Hartt, Rollin L. "The New Negro. " Independent, CV (January 15, 1921), 59-60+.

In this look at the post-World War I Negro, passing references are made to the early KKK activities in the South and the potential they could have.

F192   Haskell, Henry J. "Martial Law in Oklahoma. " Outlook, CXXXV (September 26, 1923), 133.

A report on Governor John Walton's declaration of martial law in Tulsa, Oklahoma, to curb the lawlessness of the Klan.

F193   "Heap Bad Kluxers Armed with Gun, Indian Angry, Paleface Run. " Ebony, XIII (April, 1958), 25-26+.

A report of an incident in which a band of Lumbee Indians broke up a Klan rally in North Carolina.

F194 Heath, Charles J., Jr. "A Toledo Editor Looks at the 1920's; An Interpretation of the Life of Negley D. Cochran." Northwest Ohio Quarterly, XXXIX (1967), 15-38.

A discussion of an Ohio newsman and his editorial opposition to the Ku Klux Klan.

F195 Herring, Hubert C. "The Ku Klux to the Rescue." New Republic, XXXIV (May 23, 1923), 341-42.

A satirical account of the Klan raising funds to prevent a hospital from being sold to the Catholics.

F196 Herring, Mary W. "The Why of the Ku Klux." New Republic, XXXIII (February 7, 1923), 289.

A letter to the editor, whose author sees the Klan as an outgrowth of corruption in government and a breakdown of democracy in this country.

F196a "High Court Holds Prospective Jurors May Be Questioned on Klan Membership." Harlow's Weekly, XXIII (November 29, 1924), 5.

An Oklahoma court rules that potential jurors can be asked about Klan membership in cases where KKK principles would bias the juror.

F197 Hoffman, Edwin D. "The Genesis of the Modern Movement for Equal Rights in South Carolina, 1930-1939." Journal of Negro History, XLIV (October, 1959), 346-69. (Reprinted in Sternsher, Bernard, ed. The Negro in Depression and Prelude to Revolution, 1930-1945. Chicago: Quadrangle Books, 1969.)

Some discussion of Klan attempts to prevent Negroes from registering to vote and seeking unemployment relief in South Carolina during the 1930s.

F198 "Hold Everything." Time, LIV (July 25, 1949), 12.

An Alabama grand-jury investigation of the KKK is halted when it is learned that one of the jurors had been a Klan member.

F199 Holsinger, M. Paul. "The Oregon School Controversy;

1922-25. " Pacific Historical Review, XXXVII
(August, 1968), 327-41.

A discussion of the role of the KKK in the attempt
to ban parochial schools in Oregon.

F200 "Hooded Horsemen Gallop Out of the Past in a Sudden
Revival of the KKK. " Life, (April 23, 1965), 28-
35.

A report on the recent upsurge in Klan membership and activities and a look at its leadership.

F201 "Hoods Down. " Newsweek, XXXV (April 17, 1950),
67.

A Georgia town passes an anti-mask ordinance to
combat the KKK.

F202 "Hoods Off the Klan. " Economist, CCXVII (October
26, 1965), 386+.

A report on the upcoming investigation of the KKK
by the House Un-American Activities Committee.

F203 Hoover, J. Edgar. "The Resurgent Klan. " American Bar Association Journal, LII (July, 1966), 617-
20.

The FBI director presents his views on the Klan,
given new life by opposing the civil-rights movement, and tells what the FBI can do to curb the
Klan's activities.

F204 "Houston Socialist Candidate Debates Klan Leader. "
Militant, XXXV (June 18, 1971), 12-14.

The text of a "debate" in Houston between a member of the Socialist Workers Party and the local
KKK leader.

F205 "HUAC vs. the KKK. " Senior Scholastic, LXXXVIII
(March 11, 1966), 16-17.

A report on the completion of the House Un-
American Activities Committee's investigation into
the activities of the Ku Klux Klan.

F206   Huie, William B. "Murder: The Klan on Trial."
        Saturday Evening Post, CCXXXVIII (June 19, 1965),
        86-89.

        KKK members in Georgia are acquitted for the mur-
        der of a Negro army officer driving through the
        state.

F207   Hutchinson, Paul. "The Klan Celebrates Mother's
        Day." Christian Century, XLII (May 21, 1925),
        677+.

        A report on the KKK's appearance in a New Jersey
        community.

F208   Hylden, Tom. "Grand Jury and the Klan." Space City,
        III (June 8, 1971), 7+.

        A report on a grand-jury investigation of the local
        KKK in Houston for the bombing of various offices
        and cars of left-of-center groups.

F209   "If Ever a Devil...." Time, LXXXVI (November 5,
        1965), 109.

        A local radio station in Louisiana runs afoul of the
        KKK, whose activities eventually put the station out
        of business.

F210   "The Imperial Emperor of the KKK Meets the Press."
        American Mercury, LXIX (November, 1949), 529-
        38.

        Lycurgus Spinks, Imperial Emperor of the KKK,
        answers questions on the program "Meet the Press"
        concerning the Klan's principles and activities.

F211   "Imperial Lawlessness." Outlook, CXXIX (September
        14, 1921), 46.

        Reaction to a KKK advertisement in various news-
        papers warns of possible lawlessness on the part of
        the Klan.

F212   "Indian Raid." Newsweek, LI (January 27, 1958), 27.

        A band of Lumbee Indians attack and disrupt a KKK
        rally in North Carolina.

F213   "Indiana Superior Court Issues Order Restraining Members of the Klan from Holding a Public Rally in a Certain County in Indiana." Race Relations Law Reporter, XII (Fall, 1967), 1176-78.

An Indiana court order bars the Klan from holding a public rally in Johnson County.

F214   "Indians Back at Peace and the Klan at Bay." Life, XLIV (February 3, 1958), 36-36A.

Indians in North Carolina resume their peaceful ways after disrupting a KKK rally.

F215   "Indians Rout the Klan." Commonweal, LXVII (January 31, 1958), 446.

A brief account of the Lumbee Indians' attack on a Klan rally in North Carolina.

F216   "Interview with a Former Grand Dragon." New South, XXIV (Summer, 1969), 62-79.

The former KKK head in Georgia talks about the activities of the Klan in that state.

F217   "Intolerance in Oregon." Survey, XLIX (October 15, 1922), 76-77.

A report on KKK activities in Oregon and the attempt to eliminate parochial schools.

F218   "Investigating the Ku Klux Klan." Crisis, LXXII (May, 1965), 279-80.

Editorial comment questioning the wisdom of the upcoming investigation of the KKK by the House Un-American Activities Committee.

F219   "The Invisible Empire in the Spotlight." Current Opinion, LXXI (November, 1921), 561-64.

A report on the "revival" of the KKK by William Simmons, what the Klan hopes to accomplish, and some of the opposition it has already encountered.

F220   "Invisible Government." Outlook, CXXXII (December 13, 1922), 643.

The Klan's use of secrecy is condemned as undemocratic.

F221   Irwin, Theodore. "The Klan Kicks Up Again. " American Mercury, L (August, 1940), 470-76.

A report on Klan efforts to re-establish itself in the South and across the country.

F222   " 'It Sure Was Pretty. ' " Time, LIV (November 7, 1949), 24.

Klansmen are found not guilty of assault in an Alabama trial.

F223   " 'Jack, the Klan-Fighter' in Oklahoma. " Literary Digest, LXXIX (October 20, 1923), 38-44.

A profile of Oklahoma's Governor John Walton and his campaign to rid the state of the KKK.

F224   Jackson, Charles O. "William J. Simmons: A Career in Ku Kluxism. " Georgia Historical Quarterly, L (December, 1966), 351-65.

A profile of the man who started the "revival" of the KKK after World War I, and a discussion of the growth and activities of the Klan under Simmons's leadership.

F225   Jenkins, Jay. "Again, the Klan: Old Sheets, New Victims. " Reporter, VI (March 4, 1952), 29-31.

A report on KKK activities aimed at "policing" the moral behavior of some North Carolina residents.

F226   Jenness, Linda. "Not in the Name of Feminism. " Militant, XXXIX (June 27, 1975), 11.

Some observations about disclosures of female membership and participation in the Ku Klux Klan.

F227   Johnson, Gerald W. "Fourteen Equestrian Statutes of Colonel Simmons. " Reviewer, IV (October, 1923), 20-26.

A profile of KKK leader William Simmons, whom

the author considers as the "Deliverer" of the South for establishing a group to put into effect the "prevailing social, political and religious doctrine of the region. "

F228   _____. "The Ku-Kluxer. " American Mercury, I (February, 1924), 207-11.

A look at a Klan member of the '20s and why the KKK attracted him.

F229   Johnson, Guy B. "The Race Philosophy of the Ku Klux Klan. " Opportunity, I (September, 1923), 268-69.

A discussion of the KKK's principles and a summary of its activities in support of those principles.

F230   _____. "A Sociological Interpretation of the New Ku Klux Movement. " Social Forces, I (May, 1923), 440-45.

This sociological analysis sees the KKK as: 1) a post-war phenomenon, 2) a reaction to "modernism, " and 3) a special southern phenomenon, as many Americans attempt to return to an era when things were more orderly and controllable.

F231   Johnston, Frank, Jr. "Religious and Racial Prejudices in the United States. " Current History, XX (July, 1924), 573-78.

The Klan is briefly treated and dismissed as a "modern manifestation of old prejudices against the Catholics, Jews and foreigners. "

F232   Jones, J. R. "Memories of Danbury. " Katallagete, III-IV (Winter/Spring, 1972), 26-27.

F233   Jones, Lila L. "The Ku Klux Klan in Eastern Kansas During the 1920's. " Emporia State Research Studies, XXIII (Winter, 1975), 5-41.

An analysis of KKK activities in Kansas in and out of the political arena, and the opposition the Klan encountered from Governor Henry Allen and editor William A. White.

F234   Jones, Paul. "The Ku Klux Goes Calling." New Re-
        public, LXXXV (January 8, 1936), 251.

        A local public-school teacher is reproached by the
        Klan for comments he made about communism and
        the Bible.

F235   "A Judicial Spanking for the Klan." Literary Digest,
        XCVII (April 28, 1928), 8-9.

        The Klan is criticized by a federal judge in his
        opinion on a case involving Pittsburgh Klansmen.

F236   "'Justice' by Violence." World Tomorrow, VII
        (March, 1924), 78-79.

        The accounts of a number of Klan attacks on vari-
        ous people for their anti-KKK positions.

F237   "Kashing In." Newsweek, LXVI (November 1, 1965),
        34+.

        Imperial Wizard Robert Shelton invokes the Fifth
        Amendment during his testimony before the House
        Un-American Activities Committee resulting from
        its investigation of the KKK.

F238   Kennedy, Stetson, and Evelyn M. Crowell. "The
        Ku Klux Klan." New Republic, CXIV (July 1, 1946),
        928-30.

        A report on the increase in KKK activities as it
        tries to re-establish itself and on the efforts of
        state and federal officials to stop the Klan.

F239   Kent, Frank R. "Ku Klux Klan in America." Spec-
        tator, CXXX (February 17, 1923), 279-80.

        A report on the increased activity of the Klan, as
        membership continues to rise.

F240   "Kentuckians Oppose Klan." Southern Patriot, XXXIII
        (June-July, 1975), 1.

        A report on KKK attempts to organize an anti-
        busing drive in Kentucky and the opposition the Klan
        has encountered from various sources, including the
        United Mine Workers.

F241 "Kidnapped by the Klan." Newsweek, XXXIX (February 25, 1952), 30.

The FBI arrests ten Klansmen in North Carolina for kidnapping and flogging a couple for "immorality."

F242 "Killed by Kluxers." Newsweek, XXXV (March 14, 1950), 22.

An Alabama Klansman commits suicide after participating in a raid that killed a young man.

F243 "The K. K. K." New Republic, XXVIII (September 21, 1921), 88-89.

A report on some of the disclosures about the KKK made public through an investigation by the New York World.

F244 "K. K. K. Again." New Statesman, XXII (November 10, 1923), 135-36.

A discussion of the Klan's growth and activities, using the dispute between the KKK and Governor John Walton in Oklahoma as an example.

F245 "K. K. K. : A Fading Remnant of the Past." U. S. News & World Report, LXXXI (August 2, 1976), 48.

A brief summary of some events that seem to signal a decline of the Ku Klux Klan.

F246 "KKK; Festering Sore in Chicago." Sepia, XVII (June, 1968), 60-65.

F247 "KKK Guards on the Loose at Napanoch." Worker's World, XVII (April 4, 1975), 11.

A report on Klan membership among the guards at the Napanoch state prison in New York.

F248 "K. K. K. in Florida." Newsweek, X (November 29, 1937), 18.

A report on KKK activity in Florida--in this instance a raid on a local nightclub.

F249   "KKK Offshoot Joins Houston Cops. " New Times, V
        (April 24, 1974), 2.

        A brief news report that members of a KKK spin-
        off group have become officers on the Houston po-
        lice force.

F250   "K. K. K. Over H. U. A. C. With T. K. O. " Christian
        Century, LXXXII (November 24, 1965), 1434.

        Further editorial comment from this publication
        (see F441 and F455) opposing the House Un-American
        Activities Committee's investigation of the KKK.

F251   "K. K. K. Pro and Con--Mostly Con!" Forum, LXXV
        (February, 1926), 305-08.

        Letters to the editor supporting recent articles
        against the Klan; one by Hiram Evans in support
        of the Klan; and another by William Pattangall op-
        posing the KKK.

F252   "KKK/SWP Non-Debate. " Space City, II (May 11,
        1971), 4.

        The leader of the Houston Klan appears on local
        TV with a Socialist Workers Party member to dis-
        cuss their views on various national and local is-
        sues.

F253   "K. K. K. --The White Terror of America. " New States-
        man, XVIII (October 15, 1921), 40-42.

        A discussion of the origins, organization, activities,
        rituals, and leadership of the KKK.

F254   "The Klan Acquires a College. " Literary Digest,
        LXXVIII (September 15, 1923), 42-46.

        The KKK plans to buy Valparaiso University in
        Indiana to teach "100% Americanism. "

F255   "The Klan and the Bottle. " Nation, CXVII (November
        21, 1932), 570.

        Editorial comment on the KKK and Prohibition as
        the major political issues in recent elections.

F256 "The Klan and the Candidates. " Literary Digest,
      LXXXII (September 6, 1924), 10-11.

      The 1924 Presidential candidates present their
      views on the Ku Klux Klan.

F257 "The Klan and the Democrats. " Literary Digest,
      LXXXI (June 14, 1924), 12-13.

      A report on the Klan's increasing political influence,
      and the potential problems it might cause Demo-
      cratic candidates in upcoming elections.

F258 "The Klan as a National Problem. " Literary Digest,
      LXXV (December 2, 1922), 12-13.

      A report on the Klan's growth, its activities across
      the country, and various measures that have been
      employed against it.

F259 "The Klan as an Issue. " Outlook, CXXXVIII (Septem-
      ber 3, 1924), 5-6.

      The KKK is seen as a political issue on both the
      state and national levels in the 1924 elections.

F260 "The Klan as Symptom. " Christian Century, LXXXIV
      (November 22, 1967), 1484.

      Editorial view that the Klan, whose numbers are
      increasing, is only the most visible form of racial
      prejudice, and the less visible bigots could be more
      harmful to the cause of racial equality.

F261 "The Klan as the Victim of Mob Violence. " Literary
      Digest, LXXVIII (September 8, 1923), 12-13.

      A KKK parade is attacked and disrupted outside
      Pittsburgh.

F262 "The Klan at Bay. " Current Opinion, LXXVII (Octo-
      ber, 1924), 419-22.

      Editorial comment concerning the Klan's past for-
      tune at the polls and its prospects in the upcoming
      1924 elections.

F263   "The Klan Clams Up. " New Republic, CLIII (October
          30, 1965), 11-13.

          A report on the testimony given, or not given, by
          Imperial Wizard Robert Shelton before the House
          Un-American Activities Committee.

F264   "Klan Comes to Britain: What It's All About. " U. S.
          News & World Report, LIX (July 5, 1965), 30-31.

          A report on the appearance of the KKK in Great
          Britain amid a period of increasing racial problems.

F265   "The Klan Defies a State. " Literary Digest, LXXVII
          (June 9, 1923), 12-13.

          The Klan continues its activities in New York de-
          spite the efforts of Governor Al Smith to expel the
          KKK from the state.

F266   "The Klan Enters the Campaign. " Literary Digest,
          LXXXII (July 12, 1924), 9-10.

          A report on the Klan issue at the 1924 Democratic
          National Convention and the convention's failure to
          condemn the Klan.

F266a "Klan Fight Causes Statewide Martial Law. " Harlow's
          Weekly, XXII (September 22, 1923), 8-9.

          A report on Governor John Walton's measures to
          control Klan violence in Tulsa, Oklahoma.   In-
          cluded is the text of Walton's declaration of martial
          law, which put the area under the control of the
          National Guard.

F267   "Klan for Negroes?" Newsweek, XLII (October 26,
          1953), 43.

          The United Klan, a Florida group, will allow Ne-
          groes to join its ranks in the fight against com-
          munism and desegregation (an attempt to keep the
          races pure).

F268   "The Klan Goes in for 'Face-Lifting. '" Literary Di-
          gest, XCVI (March 10, 1928), 15-16.

          The Klan removes its masks by order of Imperial

Wizard Evans, who pledges KKK opposition to Al Smith's Presidential nomination.

F269 "The Klan in Florida. " New Republic, XCI (June 9, 1937), 118.

A report of KKK activity in Tampa, Florida, where it supposedly controlled city government.

F269a "The Klan in Oklahoma Attempts to Come Back. " Harlow's Weekly, XXX (September 24, 1931), 4-7.

The Oklahoma State Fair declares "Klan Day" amid reports that the KKK is attempting a political comeback.

F270 "The Klan in Retreat and Defeat. " Independent, CXIII (August 30, 1924), 114.

A report on the decline of the Klan's political influence especially after the confrontation between the KKK and Governor John Walton in Oklahoma.

F271 "The Klan Is Guilty. " Newsweek, XXXIX (May 26, 1952), 31.

North Carolina Klansmen are convicted for kidnapping and beating a couple for "immorality. "

F272 "Klan Is in Trouble. " Life, XXXII (March 31, 1952), 44-46+.

The FBI arrests ten Klansmen in North Carolina for kidnapping.

F273 "Klan Is Outlawed in Kentucky. " Christian Century, LXIII (September 25, 1946), 1141-42.

The Klan is legally barred from "doing business" in the state of Kentucky.

F274 "The Klan Issue. " World's Work, XLVIII (October, 1924), 580.

A report on the KKK issue raised at the 1924 Democratic National Convention.

F275 "Klan Knights Put Out of Church. " Literary Digest,
      LXXVII (May 5, 1923), 37.

      Klan members are rebuffed when they enter a
      church in Pittsburgh.

F276 "Klan Kurbed. " Newsweek, XV (January 29, 1940),
      15.

      Officials in South Carolina take action to stop the
      activities of the KKK.

F277 "Klan on Kampus. " College Press Service, No. 7,
      (October 6, 1975), 6-7.

      A report that the Klan is trying to organize chap-
      ters at the University of Alabama and other south-
      ern campuses.

F278 "The Klan Rears Its Head Again. " Literary Digest,
      CXVIII (July 21, 1934), 19.

      Imperial Wizard Hiram Evans calls for a mobiliza-
      tion of the KKK to "save" the country from Soviet-
      ism, communism, and fascism.

F279 "The Klan Revives. " Commonweal, LXV (October 12,
      1956), 38.

      A very brief report on the Klan's attempts to re-
      gain its lost prestige as an aftereffect of the Su-
      preme Court's decision on school desegregation.

F280 "Klan Secrets. " Space City, III (July 6, 1971), 10+.

      A former Houston Klansman talks about the in-
      ternal affairs of the local KKK and provides copies
      of various Klan documents.

F281 "A Klan Senator from Indiana. " Literary Digest,
      LXXXVII (November 14, 1925), 16-17.

      The KKK-supported governor of Indiana appoints
      another Klan-backed politician as a U. S. Senator.

F282 "The Klan Sheds Its Hood. " New Republic, XLV
      (February 10, 1926), 310-11.

A report that the Klan is abandoning its hoods and secret oaths in an effort to continue as a political force, though its membership continues to decline.

F283 "A Klan Shock in Indiana. " Literary Digest, LXXXI (May 24, 1924), 14.

An analysis of Edward Jackson's victory in the Indiana gubernatorial race, in light of Jackson's support from the Ku Klux Klan.

F284 "Klan Victories and Defeats. " Literary Digest, LXXXIII (November 22, 1924), 16.

A survey of Klan gains and losses in recent elections.

F285 "Klan Victories in Oregon and Texas. " Literary Digest, LXXV (November 25, 1922), 12-13.

KKK-supported candidates are elected to the U. S. Senate in Texas and the governorship in Oregon.

F286 "The Klan Walks in Washington. " Literary Digest, LXXXVI (August 22, 1925), 7-8.

Imperial Wizard Evans leads 60, 000 Klan members in a parade through the nation's capital.

F287 "Klans and Councils. " New Republic, CXXXVII (September 23, 1957), 6.

Further evidence of a link between the KKK and the White Citizens Councils is found in Birmingham, Alabama.

F288 "The Klan's Challenge and the Reply. " Literary Digest, LXXIX (November 17, 1923), 32-33.

Imperial Wizard Evans says those who can't meet the KKK's standards aren't "100% American" and states that Negroes, Catholics, and Jews don't measure up; religious and ethnic publications respond to Evans's statements.

F289 "Klan's New Krisis. " Christianity Today, X (November 19, 1965), 42-43.

A report on recent Klan activities and a discussion of the KKK's use of Christian principles.

F290 "Klan's Northern Strategy to Get Integrationists. " Jet, XLI (October 14, 1971), 9.

A report that the Michigan KKK was "after" two judges (one black, one white) and an NAACP attorney for their roles in a recent school-desegregation order.

F291 "The Klan's Political Role. " Literary Digest, LXXIX (November 24, 1923), 13-14.

A survey of the KKK's political influence, where it is strong, and how it is being used.

F292 "Klansman Black?" Commonweal, XXVI (September 24, 1937), 483-84.

A discussion of the allegations about and the evidence of Hugo Black's membership in the Klan.

F293 "The Klansman's Secret. " Time, LXXXVI (November 12, 1965), 54.

A New York Klansman commits suicide when a story in the New York Times reveals he is of Jewish ancestry (see E150).

F294 "The Klansmen. " Newsweek, LXXXIV (December 16, 1974), 16-16A.

A report on the continuing existence of Klan groups in contemporary America.

F295 "Klobbered in Karolina. " Newsweek, XL (August 11, 1952), 24.

The head of the North Carolina Klan is tried and convicted for kidnapping and assault.

F296 "Kluxers on the Prowl. " Newsweek, XXXIV (July 11, 1949), 21-22.

A report on increased KKK activity in the post-World War II years in Alabama and throughout the

South and on the Klan's victims, who are mostly "poor whites. "

F297   "Knacker Knark Knipperdolling. "   Time, LXXXVII (March 4, 1966), 28.

The House Un-American Activities Committee ends its investigation of the Ku Klux Klan with few results.

F298   Knebel, Fletcher, and Clark Mollenhoff.   "Eight Klans Bring New Terror to the South. "   Look, XXI (April 30, 1957), 59-60+.

A look at the activities of the Klan in response to the first civil-rights efforts of the blacks and a profile of the leaders of the various KKK groups.

F299   Koestler, Melvin J.   "Ku Klux Klan Law. "   Cornell Law Quarterly, XIV (February, 1929), 218-22.

A survey of current laws and how they can be used in court cases involving the KKK.

F300   "Konstitutional Rites. "   Newsweek, LXVI (November 8, 1965), 34.

One of the HUAC investigators reviews various bomb-making techniques as practiced by the Klan.

F301   Kraemer, Lynn.   "Wisconsin and the KKK. "   Wisconsin Then and Now, XV (April, 1969), 1-3.

A brief summary of the KKK's organization and activities in Wisconsin.

F302   "Ku Klux and Crime. "   New Republic, XXXIII (January 17, 1923), 189-90.

A discussion of the Klan's ideology and a condemnation of its tactics, in light of the murders of two men at Mer Rouge, Louisiana.

F303   "The Ku Klux and the Election. "   Christian Century, XLI (November 20, 1924), 1496-97.

Editorial analysis of how the KKK fared in the recent national and local elections.

F304   "The Ku Klux and the Next Election. " World's Work,
       XLVI (October, 1923), 573-75.

       A discussion of the possible influence the Klan
       might have in the 1924 elections.

F305   "The Ku Klux in Politics. " Literary Digest, LXXIII
       (June 10, 1922), 15.

       A report on the Klan's involvement in political
       campaigns in Oregon and Texas, and its other
       activities elsewhere.

F306   "Ku Klux Klan. " American Federationist, XXX (No-
       vember, 1923), 919.

       The Executive Council of the American Federation
       of Labor issues an anti-Klan statement.

F307   "The Ku Klux Klan. " Canadian Forum, X (April,
       1930), 233.

       A report of a Klan incident occurring in the Canadi-
       an province of Ontario.

F308   "The Ku Klux Klan. " Catholic World, CXVI (January,
       1923), 433-43.

       A discussion of the emerging KKK, its principles,
       activities, leadership, and financial affairs.

F309   "Ku Klux Klan. " Nation, CLXII (June 8, 1946), 678.

       The Treasury Department charges the KKK for over
       $600,000 in back taxes, while the state of Georgia
       seeks to revoke the Klan's charter.

F310   "The Ku Klux Klan Again. " New Republic, CXIV
       (June 10, 1946), 822.

       A report that the House Un-American Activities
       Committee will not pursue an investigation of the
       KKK (though it did later), while officials in Georgia
       have begun efforts to rid that state of the Klan.

F311   "The Ku Klux Klan Again. " Outlook, CXXIX (Septem-
       ber 21, 1921), 79.

A brief report on the continuing growth of the KKK as it spreads its organization beyond the confines of the South.

F312   "The Ku Klux Klan and the American Clergy. "   American Ecclesiastical Review, LXX (1924), 47-58.

F313   "Ku Klux Klan: Bigotry in the Guise of Politics. " Nation, CLXXIII (August 4, 1951), 82.

A Florida Klan leader enters the race for governor despite recent "anti-mask" legislation aimed against the KKK.

F314   "Ku Klux Klan Condemned by the Religious Press. " Literary Digest, LXXI (October 1, 1921), 30-31.

A survey of anti-Klan comments by religious publications throughout the country.

F315   "Ku Klux Klan Fights St. Augustine Integration. " Sepia, XIII (September, 1964), 16-18.

F316   "The Ku Klux Klan in Germany. "   Living Age, CCCXXVII (October 17, 1925), 128.

A report that a Ku Klux Klan group has been organized in Berlin.

F317   "The Ku Klux Klan in Saskatchewan. "   Queen's Quarterly, XXXV (1928), 592-602.

F318   "Ku Klux Klan Infiltrates Houston Police Force. " Black Panther, XI (March 23, 1974), 7.

A report that a Klan group in Houston has a number of members who are on the local police force.

F319   "Ku Klux Klan on the Down Grade. "   Christian Century, XL (September 13, 1923), 1158-60.

Editorial comment predicting that the KKK's own principles will lead to its downfall.

F320   "The Ku Klux Klan on the Way Back. "   U. S. News & World Report, LVII (October 19, 1964), 51-52.

A report on increased KKK activities in the South as the Klan attempts to keep the civil-rights movement from making any gains.

F321   "Ku Klux Klan Publicity Proclaims Its Rebirth." Southern School News, VII (March, 1961), 9.

Klansmen in Louisiana tell newsmen they are regrouping and will take whatever actions circumstances demand to insure the continuation of white supremacy.

F322   "Ku Klux Klan: The Violent History of a Hooded Society." Scholastic, LXXXVII (December 2, 1965), 5-8.

A brief history of the KKK is presented as background for the investigation of the Klan by the House Un-American Activities Committee.

F323   "Ku Klux Klan Threatens Arlington Librarian." Library Journal, LXXXVII (May 15, 1962), 1866.

A report of a threatening letter from the Klan sent to the director of the Arlington, Virginia, Public Library because she refused to acquire and circulate racist material.

F324   "The Ku Klux Klan Tries a Comeback." Life, XX (May 27, 1946), 42-44.

New Klan members are initiated at a ceremony held at Stone Mountain, Georgia.

F325   "The Ku Klux Klan Tries for a Comeback." U. S. News & World Report, LXXVIII (June 23, 1975), 32-34.

The Klan tries to change its public image and broaden its support by speaking out against gun control, amnesty for Vietnam deserters, drugs, detente with Russia and China, and other contemporary issues.

F326   "The Ku Klux Klan's White Knights; They Practice a Mississippi Brand of Klansmanship." Newsweek, LXIV (December 21, 1964), 22-24.

A report on the activities of the KKK in Mississippi, where increasing pressure has been applied to curb the Klan.

F327   "The Ku Klux Victory in Texas." Literary Digest, LXXIV (August 5, 1922), 14.

A report on the victory of the Klan-supported candidate in the Texas Democratic senatorial primary and the reaction to that victory within the state.

F328   Law, Bernard F. "The Klan Still Rides." America, CX (May 30, 1964), 755.

A report of Klan activities in some Mississippi communities, including printed attacks on the Catholic Church.

F329   "Law for Others--Not for the Ku Klux Klan!" Outlook, CXXXIV (June 9, 1923), 109.

The Klan declares it will defy a New York law requiring it to register with the state and submit a membership list.

F330   Lay, Wilfrid. "Psychoanalyzing the Klan." World Tomorrow, VII (March, 1924), 79-80.

The Klan's emphases on race and secrecy are viewed as regressive elements in the KKK, which make its continued existence in a modern civilization unlikely.

F331   Lee, Kendrick. "Ku Klux Klan." Editorial Research Report, II (July 10, 1946), 449-64.

(See C25.)

F332   Leuchtenberg, William E. "A Klansman Joins the Court: The Appointment of Hugo L. Black." University of Chicago Law Review, XLI (Fall, 1973), 1-31.

A discussion of Hugo Black's appointment to the Supreme Court and the uproar that followed when it was learned that Black was a former Klan member.

F333   Linder, John. "Minn. Students Picket Speech by
       Klansman. " Militant, XXXVIII (October 25, 1974),
       23.

       An appearance by David Duke, a national KKK lead-
       er, leads to a protest by Minnesota college students.

F334   Lindsey, Ben B. "The Beast in a New Form. " New
       Republic, XLI (December 24, 1924), 121.

       A letter from a judge in Denver who was able to
       wage a successful campaign as an anti-Klan candi-
       date.

F335   _____. "My Fight with the Ku Klux Klan. " Survey,
       LIV (June 1, 1925), 271-74.

       A report on the Klan's attempt to win control over
       the Juvenile and Family Court of Denver, by the
       judge the KKK tried to remove from the bench.

F336   Lipset, Seymour M.   "An Anatomy of the Klan. "
       Commentary, XL (October, 1965), 74-83.

       (See C26.)

F337   "London's View of the Klan Row. " Literary Digest,
       LXXVII (May 19, 1923), 20.

       England observes the dispute between Klan leaders
       Simmons and Evans and feels that all the publicity
       is destroying the secrecy of the KKK.

F338   Long, Margaret. "The Imperial Wizard Explains the
       Klan. " New York Times Magazine, (July 5, 1964),
       8. (Reprinted in McCuen, Gary E. , and David L.
       Bender, eds.   The Radical Left and the Far Right;
       Fringe Groups Speak on the Problem of Race.
       Anoka, Minn. : Greenhaven Press, 1970.)

       A profile of Imperial Wizard Robert Shelton and
       some insights into the programs and goals of the
       present-day Klan.

F339   Lovejoy, Gordon W.   "In Brotherhood Week: A Look
       at the South. " New York Times Magazine, (Febru-
       ary 17, 1957), 13+.

A look at the Klan trying to "revive" itself in the South and some of the tactics it is employing to counter desegregation attempts.

F340   Lynn, Alexander.   "Boston Blacks Face Racist Gangs. " Guardian, XXVI (October 9, 1974), 7.

A report on Klan activities in the Boston area to prevent the busing of black children to all-white schools.

F341   "Ma Ferguson and the K. K. K. "   New Statesman, XXIII (October 4, 1924), 728-29.

A report on Miriam "Ma" Ferguson and her successful campaign against a KKK candidate for the governorship of Texas.

F342   McConville, Edward.   "Portrait of a Klansman;   The Prophetic Voice of C. P. Ellis. "   Nation, CCXVII (October 15, 1973), 361-66.

A profile of C. P. Ellis, a KKK leader in Durham, North Carolina, and his somewhat unique way of looking at the racial situation in this country and how it should be handled.

F343   McLean, Phillip J.   "Klan Reborn on Stone Mountain. " Christian Century, LXIII (June 5, 1946), 726.

A cross-burning ceremony on Stone Mountain signals the Klan's return to Georgia.

F344   McMillan, George.   "The Klan Scourges Old St. Augustine. "   Life, LVI (June 26, 1964), 21.

Klan members confront civil-rights protesters led by Martin Luther King, Jr. , in St. Augustine, Florida.

F345   McWilliams, Carey.   "The Klan: Post-War Model. " Nation, CLXIII (December 14, 1946), 691-94.

As the state of Georgia tries to revoke the KKK's charter, Klan activities begin to increase across the country.

F346   "Malice Toward Some. " Newsweek, LXVII (April 11, 1966), 39-40.

Mississippi's KKK leader and other Klansmen are arrested by the FBI for the murder of a local NAACP official.

F347   Marriner, Gerald L.   "Klan Politics in Colorado. " Journal of the West, XV (January, 1976), 76-101.

A discussion of the development, leadership, and activities of the KKK in Colorado especially in the political arena, where the Klan was able to exercise considerable control.

F348   Martin, Harold H.   "The Truth About the Klan Today. " Saturday Evening Post, CCXXII (October 22, 1949), 17-18+.

A look at the statutes, organization, and activities of the post-World War II Ku Klux Klan.

F349   Martin, Harold H. , and Kenneth Fairly.   "Ku Klux Klan: We Got Nothing to Hide. " Saturday Evening Post, CCXXXVIII (January 30, 1965), 26-33+.

A look at the KKK, its image in the 1960s, its activities in opposing the civil-rights movement, and its leadership under Imperial Wizard Robert Shelton.

F350   Martin, John B.   "Beauty and the Beast; The Downfall of D. C. Stephenson, Grand Dragon of the Indiana K. K. K. "   Harper's Magazine, CLXXXIX (September, 1944), 319-29.

The story of David Stephenson's downfall as the head of the KKK in Indiana; Stephenson was found guilty of the murder of a young girl he had earlier assaulted.   The girl's death-bed confession is included.

F351   "The Masked Floggers of Tulsa. "   Literary Digest, LXXVIII (September 22, 1923), 17.

Governor John Walton of Oklahoma declares martial law in Tulsa in an effort to halt an outbreak of floggings and lawlessness caused by the KKK.

F352   "Mayor Curley's [Boston, Mass.] Ringing Letter on
       Ku Klux Klan. "   City Record, XV (January 27,
       1923), 93.

       In a letter to a Texas attorney, the mayor of Bos-
       ton presents his views on how and why the KKK
       should be abolished.

F353   Mazzulla, Fred, and Jo Mazzulla.   "A Klan Album. "
       Colorado Magazine, XLII (Spring, 1965), 93-113.

       A collection of photographs from the KKK days in
       Colorado.

F354   Mecklin, John M.   "Ku Klux Klan and the Democratic
       Tradition. "   American Review, II (May-June, 1924),
       241-51.

       An examination of how the KKK can uphold the
       "democratic tradition" with its reliance on secrecy
       and masks to further its goals and how the Klan
       can claim to be "100% American" while it supports
       anti-Catholic and other un-American principles.

F355   Meier, August, and Elliott Rudwick.   "Early Boycotts
       of Segregated Schools: The Case of Springfield,
       Ohio, 1922-23. "   American Quarterly, XX (Winter,
       1968), 744-58.

       A discussion of the fact that various teachers and
       school officials involved in the Fulton school con-
       troversy were Klan members and received Klan
       support in local elections.

F356   Melching, Richard.   "The Activities of the Ku Klux
       Klan in Anaheim, California, 1923-1925. "   Southern
       California Quarterly, LVI (Summer, 1974), 175-96.

       A discussion of KKK activities in this southern
       California community, where the Klan tried to gain
       political control, although it "began after the peak
       of nativist hysteria had been reached. "   The au-
       thor credits this KKK group as being "almost com-
       pletely non-violent and law abiding. "

F357   Mellard, James M.   "Racism, Formula, and Popular

Fiction. " Journal of Popular Culture, V (Summer, 1971), 10-37.

(See C31.)

F358   Mellett, Lowell. "Klan and Church. " Atlantic, CXXXII (November, 1923), 586-92.

A discussion of the situation that allowed the Klan to gain such a stronghold in Indiana.

F359   "Mer Rouge Murders Unpunished. " Literary Digest, LXXVI (March 31, 1923), 10-11.

A Louisiana grand jury fails to return indictments against Klan members involved in the murders of two men at Mer Rouge. KKK leaders claim the jury's action as a vindication of the Klan.

F360   Merritt, Dixon. "Klan and Anti-Klan in Indiana. " Outlook, CXLIV (December 8, 1926), 465-69.

A report on the Klan influence in Indiana, KKK leader David Stephenson, and forces within the state that oppose the Klan.

F361   _____. "The Klan on Parade. " Outlook, CXL (August 19, 1925), 553-54.

A report on the KKK parade through Washington, D. C.

F362   Merz, Charles. "The New Ku-Klux Klan. " Independent, CXVIII (February 12, 1927), 179-80+.

In an attempt to bolster its declining membership, the KKK turns from religious to political issues, condemning the World Court, opposing cancellation of the European war debts, and supporting high standards of morality and the Volstead Act (Prohibition), as well as engaging in more "social" activities.

F363   Middlebrooks, Acton E. "Alabama Votes to Unmask Klan. " Christian Century, LXVI (July 20, 1949), 871.

A report of a recent law in Alabama that makes the wearing of masks by the KKK or any group illegal.

F364   Miller, Robert M.   "A Note on the Relationship Between the Protestant Churches and the Revived Ku Klux Klan. "   Journal of Southern History, XXII (August, 1956), 355-68.

An examination of the relationship between the KKK and Protestant churches, citing examples of anti-Klan articles that appeared in Protestant publications during the '20s and other anti-Klan measures on the part of Protestant congregations.

F365   _____.   "The Social Attitudes of the American Methodists, 1919-29. "   Religion in Life, XXVII (Spring, 1958), 185-98.

References are made to examples of Methodist opposition to the Klan.

F366   "Ministers Denounce Georgia Klan. "   Christian Century, LXVI (January 5, 1949), 6.

Georgia Methodists denounce the Ku Klux Klan as an "anti-Christian mob. "

F367   "Miss KKK. "   Newsweek, XXXII (December 20, 1948), 22.

A small child is inducted into the KKK in Georgia.

F368   "Mr. White Challenges the Klan. "   Outlook, CXXXVIII (October 1, 1924), 154.

William Allen White will run for the governorship of Kansas on an anti-Klan ticket.

F369   Mitchell, T.   "FBI Helped Klan Gun Down Civil Rights Fighters. "   Worker's World, XVII (December 12, 1975), 5.

A former FBI informer presents testimony that the FBI had prior knowledge of the murder of civil-rights worker Viola Liuzzo.

F370   Moore, Samuel T.   "A Klan Kingdom Collapses; How
       the Kleagles Collected the Cash; Consequences of
       the Klan in Indiana." Independent, CXIII (Decem-
       ber 6, 1924), 473-75; (December 13, 1924), 517-
       19; and (December 20, 1924), 534-36.

       A three-part report on KKK activities in Indiana,
       including its political influence under the leadership
       of David Stephenson, how the Klan attracted mem-
       bers and kept its treasury full, and what the Klan's
       presence means for Indiana.

F371   "More Texas Klansmen Indicted." Militant, XXXV
       (June 25, 1971), 5.

       A report on a Houston grand jury's actions against
       KKK members in connection with bombings and oth-
       er acts against the Socialist Workers Party and
       other left-wing groups in that community.

F372   Moseley, Clement C.   "The Political Influence of the
       Ku Klux Klan in Georgia, 1915-1925." Georgia
       Historical Quarterly, LVII (Summer, 1973), 235-55.

       A study of the KKK's role in Georgia politics on
       both the state and national levels, who the Klan
       supported, and why.

F373   Mugleston, William F.   "Julian Harris, the Georgia
       Press, and the Ku Klux Klan." Georgia Historical
       Quarterly, LIX (Fall, 1975), 284-95.

       A study of the activities of Julian Harris, whose
       newspaper was the first in Georgia to take an anti-
       Klan position, and other papers in the state that
       eventually came to oppose the KKK.

F374   "The Murders of Mer Rouge." Literary Digest,
       LXXVI (January 13, 1923), 10-12.

       The Klan is suspected in the murders of two men
       in Mer Rouge, Louisiana.

F375   Murphy, Paul L.   "Sources and Nature of Intolerance
       in the 1920's." Journal of American History, LI
       (June, 1964), 60-76.

Brief mention of the Klan is made in regard to their anti-Catholic and anti-Semitic ideology.

F376   "Mutiny in the Invisible Empire. " Independent, CXVI (January 16, 1926), 58-59.

Some 600 KKK members resign from the Klan chapter in New Haven, Connecticut, and issue an anti-Klan statement in the process.

F377   " 'My Kountry'--Klonsel's Kreed. " Newsweek, LXV (May 17, 1965), 41.

The text of attorney Matt Murphey's summation in his defense of a Klan member accused of murdering civil-rights worker Viola Liuzzo.

F378   Myers, William S.   "Know Nothing and Ku Klux Klan. " North American Review, CCXIX (January, 1924), 1-7.

A comparison of the principles and goals of the KKK with those of the Know Nothing Party of the 1850s.

F379   _____. "The Ku Klux Klan of Today. " North American Review, CCXXIII (June, 1926), 304-09.

The Klan is viewed as an organization on the decline because of its denial of racial and religious freedom.

F380   "The Natives Are Restless. " Time, LXXI (January 27, 1958), 20.

The Lumbee Indians of North Carolina attack and disrupt a Klan rally.

F381   Nelson, Jack.   "Terror in Mississippi. " New South, XXIII (Fall, 1968), 41-57.

Two Klan members are shot in an attempt to bomb the home of a Jewish businessman in Mississippi. A report on KKK activities in Mississippi is included.

F382   Nelson, Llewellyn.   "The K. K. K. for Boredom. "

New Republic, XLI (January 14, 1925), 196-98.

A sympathetic view of the KKK in Oklahoma that claims that many deeds performed by the Klan were actually committed by others.

F383   Neuringer, Sheldon. "Governor Walton's War on the Ku Klux Klan: An Episode in Oklahoma History, 1923 to 1924." Chronicles of Oklahoma, XLV (1967), 153-79.

A discussion of Oklahoma governor John Walton's activities in attempting to rid the state of the Klan, which resulted in Walton's impeachment.

F384   Nevin, David. "Strange, Tight Little Town, Loath to Admit Complicity." Life, LVII (December 18, 1964), 38-39.

The story of Philadelphia, Mississippi, a town under considerable Klan influence and the site of the murder of three civil-rights workers.

F385   "New Ku Klux Klan Activity." Scholastic, XXXVI (May 13, 1940), 2-3.

A brief report of renewed activity by the KKK in Georgia.

F386   "New York's Anti-Klan Outburst." Literary Digest, LXXV (December 23, 1922), 31-32.

A report on KKK activities in New York and the opposition the Klan has confronted there.

F387   "Next Step: Button-Down Robes." Time, LXXXIII (May 1, 1964), 23.

The Klan tries to gain some respectability through the leadership of Imperial Wizard Robert Shelton.

F388   Nicholson, Meredith. "Hoosier Letters and the Ku Klux." Bookman, LXVII (March, 1928), 7-11.

A look at the extent to which the Klan controlled politics in Indiana.

F389 "Nightmare on Pine Mountain. " Time, LI (March 22, 1948), 24-25.

Three Georgia newsmen are assaulted by Klan members as they try to report on a KKK initiation meeting.

F390 "No Place for Fanatics. " Collier's National Weekly, C (October 23, 1937), 74.

A call for the resignation of Hugo Black from the Supreme Court because of his Ku Klux Klan affiliations.

F391 " 'Nobody Turned Me 'Round. ' " Time, LXXXVI (October 15, 1965), 31-32.

Negroes and the Klan square off in Natchez, Mississippi, with demonstrations and counter-demonstrations.

F392 "North Carolina Superior Court Issues a Restraining Order Prohibiting the Ku Klux Klan from Holding Rallies in Robeson County, North Carolina Which Intimidate Indians and Negroes and Create Civil Strife, Tension and Riots. " Race Relations Law Reporter, XI (Fall, 1966), 1162-65.

A North Carolina court order bars the Klan from holding a public rally in Robeson County.

F393 Northcott, Karen. "Jimmy Dale Hutto Convicted; Guilty on 3 Counts. " Space City, III (September 14, 1971), 4.

Houston Klansman is found guilty on bombing conspiracy and firearms violation charges.

F394 Northcott, Karen, and Victoria Smith. "Hutto, Would This Man Blow Up a Train. " Space City, III (September 7, 1971), 3-5.

A profile of a Houston Klansman on trial for a bombing incident.

F395 Oates, Stephen B. "Boom Oil! Oklahoma Strikes It Rich! " American West, V (January, 1968), 11-15+.

The Klan is viewed in an effort to bring some sem-
blance of law and order and enforcement of strict
moral conduct into the Tulsa oil fields of 1921.

F396 O'Brien, Kenneth B. , Jr. "Education, Americaniza-
tion and the Supreme Court; The 1920's. " American Quarterly, XIII (1961), 161-71.

Brief mention of the Klan in regard to its role in
the passage of the 1922 Oregon law that banned
parochial schools.

F397 "Oklahoma Kingless, Not Klanless. " Literary Digest,
LXXIX (December 8, 1923), 9.

Oklahoma Governor John Walton has been impeached, but the question of the Klan's involvement
in state government remains.

F397a "Oklahoma's Klan War from Over the Border. " Harlow's Weekly, XXII (September 22, 1924), 4-5.

A survey of recent editorial comments concerning
the Klan's "war" in Oklahoma, and how newspapers
from states neighboring Oklahoma condemn Governor Walton for his actions against the KKK, while
editorials from other parts of the country praise
Walton's efforts.

F398 "Oklahoma's Uncivil Civil War. " Literary Digest,
LXXVIII (September 29, 1923), 10-11.

A further report on the events in Oklahoma that
led Governor John Walton to declare martial law in
an effort to stop the Klan and what has happened
since that time.

F399 "Oscar Underwood's Great Service. " World's Work,
XLVIII (July, 1924), 242-43.

A brief tribute to politician Oscar Underwood for
publicly denouncing the KKK as a threat and a menace to the country.

F400 Ottley, Roi. "I Met the Grand Dragon. " Nation,
CLXIX (July 2, 1949), 10-11.

A profile of the KKK's leader, Grand Dragon Samuel Green, and what the Klan represents, by a Negro correspondent who interviewed Green.

F401 "Our Own Secret Fascists. " Nation, CXV (November 15, 1922), 514.

Editorial comment on the Klan's recent growth and political successes and measures being taken in some states to curb the KKK influence.

F402 "Out of the Cave. " Time, XLVII (June 3, 1946), 25.

Klan activities against Jews and Negroes increase in Los Angeles as World War II ends.

F403 Owens, John W.   "Does the Senate Fear the K. K. K. ?" New Republic, XXXVIII (December 26, 1923), 113-14.

The Senate is faced with the question of charges against the Klan-backed candidate from Texas for violation of election laws.

F404 Papanikolas, Helen Z.   "Tragedy and Hate. " Utah Historical Quarterly, XXXVIII (Spring, 1970), 176-81.

The KKK crusades against Greek immigrants in Utah during the 1920s.

F405 Pattangall, William R.   "Is the Ku Klux Un-American?" Forum, LXXIV (September, 1925), 321-32.

The KKK and the potential danger it holds for this country are discussed by an anti-Klan Democrat from Maine.

F406 Patton, R. A.   "A Ku Klux Klan Reign of Terror. " Current History, XXVIII (April, 1928), 51-55.

A discussion of the Klan and some of the acts it committed during the 1920s.

F407 Paul, Justus F.   "The Ku Klux Klan in the Midwest: A Note on the 1936 Nebraska Elections. " North

Dakota Quarterly, XXXIX (Autumn, 1971), 64-70.

Republicans in Nebraska accept the aid of the KKK in their opposition to President Franklin Roosevelt and Senator George Norris.

F408   Payne, George H.   "Does the Ku Klux Need the Jew?" Forum, LXXIV (December, 1925), 915-17.

Some thoughts about the Klan as a political power and its future in this country.

F409   Percy, Leroy.   "The Modern Ku Klux Klan. "   Atlantic, CXXX (July, 1922), 122-28.

A discussion of conditions within the country that have led to the growth of the KKK.   The principles and organization of the Klan are also presented, as are illustrations of the Klan's activities.

F410   Perlmutter, Nathan.   "Bombing in Miami; Anti-Semitism and the Segregationists. "   Commentary, XXV (June, 1958), 498-503.

A look at the Klan's anti-Semitism against the backdrop of the bombing of a synagogue in Florida.

F411   "Pink Ballots for the Ku Klux Klan. "   Outlook, CXXXVII (June 25, 1924), 306-09.

A discussion and analysis of the response by Klan members to an opinion poll sponsored by the Outlook to see how they stand on various issues.

F412   "Playboy Interview: Robert Shelton. "   Playboy, XII (August, 1965), 45-46+.

Imperial Wizard Robert Shelton explains the Klan's principles and activities in the 1960s.

F413   "Playing with Fire. "   Time, LIII (January 3, 1949), 42.

The KKK tries to intimidate a Georgia newspaper editor when his paper calls for an investigation of the Klan.

F414 Powell, John. "The Klan Un-Klandestine. " Nation, CLXXIII (September 29, 1951), 254-56.

Reflections on a North Carolina Klan rally and the image the KKK is trying to present.

F415 "The Protectors. " Time, LXXXVIII (July 8, 1966), 20.

Three Klansmen are tried in a U. S. District Court for their part in the murder of a Negro Army Reserve officer in Georgia.

F416 "Protectors of Womanhood. " Time, LI (February 16, 1948), 26.

The KKK burns crosses in Georgia and vows to "protect white womanhood. "

F417 "Protestants Disowning the Ku Klux. " Literary Digest, LXXV (November 25, 1922), 33.

A statement from an official church group denounces the KKK and similar organizations and says such groups have no right to speak in the name of Protestantism.

F418 "Public Hearings in Probe of Ku Klux Klan Announced." Congressional Quarterly Weekly Report, XXIII (October 15, 1965), 2095-97.

Recent acts of violence by the KKK lead to an investigation of the Klan by the House Un-American Activities Committee.

F419 "The Public's Rating of Controversial Organizations. " Gallup Opinion Index, LXII (August, 1970), 10-22.

The KKK is rated unfavorable in a nationwide Gallup poll.

F420 "Quaint Customs and Methods of the Ku Klux Klan. " Literary Digest, LXXIV (August 5, 1922), 44-52.

A discussion of the KKK's growth and influence across the country, and a survey of its recent activities, especially in Oklahoma and California.

F421   Racine, Philip N. "The Ku Klux Klan, Anti-Catholicism, and Atlanta's Board of Education, 1916-1927." Georgia Historical Quarterly, LVII (Spring, 1973), 63-75.

The Klan pressures the Atlanta school board to dismiss Catholic teachers as part of its anti-Catholic crusade.

F422   Rambow, Charles. "The Ku Klux Klan in the 1920's: A Concentration on the Black Hills." South Dakota History, IV (1973), 63-81.

A discussion of the general organization and principles of the KKK, with specific examples of Klan activity in the Black Hills area of South Dakota.

F423   "The Reformation of Herrin." Literary Digest, LXXXVI (August 1, 1925), 28-29.

The KKK's hold over Herrin, Illinois, is broken, as residents are persuaded to put aside their guns and obey the law.

F424   Reed, Roy. "The Deacons, Too, Ride by Night." New York Times Magazine, (August 15, 1965), 10-11+.

A Negro group puts up armed resistance to the KKK in Louisiana.

F425   "The Reign of the Tar Bucket." Literary Digest, LXX (August 27, 1921), 12-13.

The Klan is condemned in newspapers across the country for its recent activities, especially in Texas.

F426   Reinholz, Mary. "A Visit to a KKK Koffee Klatch in Upstate New York." New Dawn, I (September, 1976), 36-41.

Female Klan members in New York present their rationale for belonging to the KKK.

F427   Ring, Harry. "Houston Election Campaign Puts Socialists on the Map." Militant, XXXV (December 24, 1971), 12-13.

The Houston Klan aggressively responds to a Socialist candidate's campaign for mayor.

F428   "The Riot at Niles. " Outlook, CXXXVIII (November 12, 1924), 396.

The state militia is called out to oppose the KKK in Ohio.

F429   "The Rise and Fall of the K. K. K. " New Republic, LIII (November 30, 1927), 33-34.

A report on the Klan's declining status in a number of states and of legal proceedings conducted against many Klan members.

F430   "The Rise and Fall of the Ku Klux Klan. " Outlook, CXXXVIII (October 15, 1924), 237-38.

A report that the Klan is losing some of its influence on both the local and national scenes.

F431   Roberts, Waldo. "The Ku-Kluxing of Oregon. " Outlook, CXXXIII (March 14, 1923), 490-91.

A report on the Klan's successful political activities in Oregon.

F432   Rork, C. M. "A Defense of the Klan. " New Republic, XXXVII (December 5, 1923), 44.

A Dallas reader writes to uphold the Klan, claiming that its success is due to "persistent, effective advertising. "

F433   Rosenberg, Harold. "The Art World: Liberation from Detachment. " New Yorker, XLVI (November 7, 1970), 136+.

A review of artist Philip Guston's show of paintings depicting the KKK.

F434   Rovere, Richard H. "The Klan Rides Again. " Nation, CL (April 6, 1940), 445-46.

Murders and beatings for "immoral conduct" in Georgia signal a return of KKK activity.

F435   Ruark, Henry G. "Fear Klan Revival in the Carolinas."
        Christian Century, LXXV (February 26, 1958), 257.

        A report of increased KKK activities in North and
        South Carolina; however, the Klan is finding little
        support for its efforts.

F436   "Same Old HUAC." Nation, CCI (November 1, 1965),
        290-91.

        Editorial comment concerning the investigation of
        the KKK by the House Un-American Activities Com-
        mittee.

F437   Schaefer, Richard T. "The Ku Klux Klan: Continuity
        and Change." Phylon, XXXII (Summer, 1971), 143-
        57.

        (See C42.)

F438   Schardt, Arlie. "A Mississippi Mayor Fights the
        Klan." Reporter, XXXIV (January 27, 1966), 39-
        40.

        The mayor of Laurel, Mississippi, tries to halt
        an outbreak of Klan-induced violence.

F439   Schieffelin, William J. "The Most Unforgettable Char-
        acter I've Met." Reader's Digest, LVII (Novem-
        ber, 1950), 25-28. Reprinted in Negro Digest, IX
        (February, 1951), 66-68.

        The Klan threatens action when it learns the Vet-
        erans Administration will build a hospital in Tus-
        kegee, Alabama, for Negro war veterans and staff
        it with Negro doctors and nurses.

F440   Scott, Martin J. "Catholics and the Ku Klux Klan."
        North American Review, CCXXIII (June, 1926),
        268-81.

        A Catholic leader responds to some anti-Catholic
        statements made by the Klan.

F441   "Sending a Goose to Catch a Fox." Christian Century,
        LXXXII (April 14, 1965), 453.

Editorial comment questioning that anything will result from the House Un-American Activities Committee's investigation of the KKK.

F442   Shankman, Arnold. "Julian Harris and the Ku Klux Klan. " Mississippi Quarterly, XXVIII (Spring, 1975), 147-69.

A discussion of Georgia newspaper editor Julian Harris and his crusade to expose the Klan as an organization of prejudice, violence, and hatred.

F443   "Shed a Tear for the Klan. " Nation, CXIX (October 8, 1924), 351-52.

The KKK is credited with saving "America from falling into the hands of a dictatorial fascism. "

F444   "Sheet, Sugar Sack & Cross. " Time, LI (March 15, 1948), 29.

The Georgia Klan keeps registered Negroes from voting.

F445   "Sheeted Jerks. " Nation, CLXIX (July 2, 1949), 2.

KKK activity against white citizens leads the American Legion in Alabama to oppose the Klan.

F446   Shepard, William G. "Fighting the K. K. K. on Its Home Ground. " Leslie's Magazine, CXXXIII (October 15, 1921), 508-11+.

A discussion of the efforts of newsmen Julian Harris and Thomas Loyless and their editorial campaign against the KKK in Columbus, Georgia.

F447   _____. "How I Put Over the Klan. " Collier's National Weekly, LXXXII (July 14, 1928), 5-7+; (July 21, 1928), 8-9+; and (July 28, 1928), 8-9+.

A profile of William Simmons, Imperial Wizard and founder of the "revived" KKK, as he tells how he started the "Invisible Empire. "

F448   _____. "Indiana's Mystery Man. " Collier's National Weekly, LXXIX (January 8, 1927), 8-9+.

A profile of David Stephenson, Indiana Klan leader; his influence on the state's political scene; and his trial for the murder of a young girl.

F449   . "Ku Klux Koin. " Collier's National Weekly, LXXXII (July 21, 1928), 8-9.

A discussion of Imperial Wizard Simmons's plan to establish a KKK "secret service" of 50, 000 men throughout the country. Simmons, however, lost control of the Klan before the spy network could be established.

F450   . "The Whip Hand. " Collier's National Weekly, LXXXI (January 7, 1928), 8-9+.

A discussion of the KKK's strength in Alabama and attempts by state officials to control the Klan, against the backdrop of the Klan's whipping of a white couple.

F451   . "The Whip Wins. " Collier's National Weekly, LXXXI (January 14, 1928), 10-11+.

A report that indictments against KKK members who had confessed to whippings were dropped when a pro-Klan jury returned a verdict of acquittal.

F452   Sherman, Richard B. "Republicans and Negroes: The Lessons of Normalcy. " Phylon, XXVII (Spring, 1966), 63-79.

A discussion of the KKK's political influence and the Republican Party's attitude toward the Klan, especially during the 1924 Presidential campaign.

F453   Sherrill, Robert. "Expose of Tedium, Terror and Fiscal Tricks at HUAC. " New South, XXI (Winter, 1966), 57-63.

A report on the investigation of the KKK by the House Un-American Activities Committee and some of its findings.

F454   . "A Look Inside the Invisible Empire. " New South, XXIII (Spring, 1968), 4-30.

A report on the current status of the KKK and some of the Klan's recent activities.

F455   "Shooting at the Klan but Wounding the Negro." Christian Century, LXXXII (September 22, 1965), 1149.

A report on a petition drawn up by Martin Luther King, Jr., and the Southern Christian Leadership Conference and signed by various civil-rights and religious leaders. The petition urges opposition to the forthcoming HUAC investigation of the KKK.

F456   "Shots in the Shadows." Newsweek, XLIX (February 4, 1957), 26+.

An Alabama Klansman is shot by a KKK leader when his control of the local Klan unit is questioned.

F457   Shumaker, W. A. "The Ku Klux Klan in Court." Law Notes, XXVII (March, 1924), 225-27.

A survey of recent court cases throughout the country that in some way involve the Ku Klux Klan.

F458   Silverman, Joseph. "The Ku Klux Klan a Paradox." North American Review, CCXXIII (June, 1926), 282-91.

The role of the KKK in American society is questioned and refuted.

F459   Singer, Stu. "Armed Klansmen Threaten Socialists." Militant, XXXIX (March 7, 1975), 28.

The KKK, aided and abetted by the Houston police, harass Socialist political candidates.

F460   Sitton, Claude. "Once More--The KKK." New York Times Magazine, (August 11, 1963), 8-9+.

A pictorial essay on the latest attempts by the Klan to increase its membership.

F461   Skinner, R. Dana. Is the Ku Klux Klan, Katholik?" Independent, CXI (November 24, 1923), 242-43.

The theory is put forth that the KKK seeks to play an old game, but with new rules, and it attacks Jews and Catholics because they still retain the old rules.

F462   Sloan, Charles W., Jr.   "Kansas Battles the Invisible Empire: The Legal Ouster of the KKK from Kansas, 1922-1927." Kansas Historical Quarterly, XL (Autumn, 1974), 393-409.

A study of the attempts of Governor Henry Allen and others to force the Ku Klux Klan out of Kansas.

F463   Smith, Baxter.   "The Klan Rides at Napanoch." Militant, XXXIX (January 24, 1975), 11.

A report that the KKK is active in harassing Negro prisoners at the Napanoch state prison in New York.

F464   _____. "Klan Rides at Napanoch (II)." Militant, XXXIX (April 4, 1975), 24.

Further evidence is presented to suggest the KKK's presence at the Napanoch state prison in New York.

F465   Smith, Norman.   "The Ku Klux Klan in Rhode Island." Rhode Island History, XXXVII (May, 1978), 35-45.

A discussion of the presence of the KKK in Rhode Island; its anti-alien, anti-Catholic, and anti-Semitic campaigns; and its eventual disappearance from the scene.

F466   Smith, Robert B.   "Klan Spooks in Congress." Independent, CXVI (June 19, 1926), 718-19+.

The KKK, through the elected officials it supported, is keeping its eye on national affairs, as it makes sure that the "Klan bloc" in Congress supports the principles of the "Invisible Empire."

F467   Smith, Victoria.   "Lowe-Down." Space City, II (June 1, 1971), 6.

A profile of a Houston KKK member, who is suspected in the bombing and harassing of leftist and liberal groups.

F468   Smith, William. "William Jennings Bryan and Racism. "
        Journal of Negro History, LIV (April, 1969), 127-
        49.

        A discussion of Bryan (who was memorialized by
        the KKK) and his relationship with the Klan.

F469   Snell, William R. "Fiery Crosses in the Roaring
        Twenties: Activities of the Revised Klan in Ala-
        bama, 1915-1930. " Alabama Review, XXIII (Octo-
        ber, 1970), 256-76.

        A discussion of the KKK in Alabama, its growth
        and activities, especially in "policing" the morals
        and patriotism of the community.

F470   "Solemn but Undignified Penguins. " Nation, CXVI
        (January 3, 1923), 6.

        Editorial question of what to do with a group who
        commits unlawful acts in the name of country and
        constitution, not against them.

F471   Sonnichsen, C. L. , and M. G. McKinney. "El Paso--
        From War to Depression. " Southwestern Historical
        Quarterly, LXXIV (January, 1971), 357-71.

        A discussion of KKK activities during the 1920s in
        the Texas border town of El Paso.

F472   "South Carolina Race War. " New Republic, CXXIII
        (September 11, 1950), 9.

        The Klan attempts to drive Negroes away from a
        South Carolina resort area.

F473   "Southern Exposure. " Newsweek, LXXII (November 25,
        1968), 111-12.

        A former Klan member discusses the tactics and
        goals of the KKK on a New Orleans television sta-
        tion.

F474   "Southern Liberals Oppose Klan. " Christian Century,
        LXIII (June 5, 1946), 726.

        A report on the reaction to attempts by the KKK to
        regain a position of prominence in the South.

F475   "Southern Reaction to Arrest of Klansmen. "   Nation,
        CLXXIV (March 8, 1952), 215.

        FBI arrest of ten Klansmen elicits a positive re-
        sponse from the people of North Carolina.

F476   Spivak, John L.   "Unmasking the KKK. "   New Masses,
        (April 21, 1942), 4-9.

        A report on KKK activities in the Detroit area, in-
        cluding Klan strength in organized labor and com-
        ments from Imperial Wizard James Colescott.

F477   Stacy, Kay.   "FBI Helped Klan. "   Worker's Power,
        No. XXXIX (December 12, 1975), 1+.

        A former FBI informant reveals how FBI activity
        aided the Klan in its anti-civil-rights activities.

F478   Stephens, Harold W.   "Mask and Lash in Crenshaw. "
        North American Review, CCXXV (April, 1928),
        435-42.

        Reports of KKK activities, especially floggings in
        Alabama, where officials were unable to obtain in-
        dictments against Klan members.

F479   Stewart, Ted.   "The KKK Takes to TV Plugs. "   Sepia,
        XXV (March, 1976), 82.

        A report on the Klan's use of media commercials
        to help increase its membership.

F480   Stockbridge, Frank P.   "The Ku Klux Klan Revival. "
        Current History, XIV (April, 1921), 19-25.

        A discussion of the principles and activities of the
        KKK, as the "revived" Klan attempts to go beyond
        the borders of the South and seek members in the
        North and West.

F481   Stone, Elizabeth.   "KKK Scum in Boston: 'Real Issue
        Is Niggers. ' "   Militant, XXXVIII (October 18, 1974),
        4.

        A report of the KKK's intervention into the school-
        desegregation issue in Boston.

F482   "The Strange 'Invasion.'"   Newsweek, XLIX (May 13, 1957), 58.

> The KKK attempts to establish itself in England to help maintain white supremacy and combat communism and social evils.

F483   "Subpoena the Klan."   America, XCVI (February 9, 1957), 520.

> A review of the KKK situation in Mobile, Alabama, and a call for shining some light on Klan membership by questioning before a Congressional committee.

F484   Sullivan, Mark.   "Midsummer Politics and Primaries." World's Work, XLIV (July, 1922), 296-302.

> A brief report on the Klan as an issue in Texas politics.

F485   Swart, Stanley L.   "A Memo on Cross-Burning--And Its Implications."   Northwest Ohio Quarterly, XLIII (1971), 70-74.

> An analysis of a memo concerning the proper procedure to follow when burning crosses.   This memo from a Klan chapter in Dayton, Ohio, provides some insight into the internal operation of a local KKK unit.

F486   Sweeney, Charles P.   "The Great Bigotry Merger." Nation, CXV (July 5, 1922), 8-10.

> A discussion of the KKK and its recent activities, including a number of examples of how the Klan works, in light of attempts to form a group called the Great American Fraternity, which would include the KKK and other such organizations.

F487   Swertfeger, Jack, Jr.   "Anti-Mask and Anti-Klan Laws." Journal of Public Laws, I (Spring, 1952), 182-97.

> A discussion of recent state laws, including those in some southern states that are aimed against the Ku Klux Klan by forbidding the wearing of masks.

F488   "Talent Rewarded: Mr. Justice Black." Catholic
        World, CXLVI (November, 1937), 129-34.

        Editorial comment concerning Hugo Black's past
        membership in the KKK and his recent appointment
        to the Supreme Court.

F489   Tannenbaum, Frank.   "Ku Klux Klan, Its Social Ori-
        gin in the South." Century, CV (April, 1923),
        873-82.

        This analysis of the KKK's "rebirth" after World
        War I cites three factors that fostered the Klan
        in the South: 1) the habit of using violence to de-
        fend social status, 2) social gains made by Negroes
        during the war, and 3) economic gains by Negroes
        to support the social gains.

F490   Taylor, Alva W.   "Klan Seen Trying for a Comeback."
        Christian Century, LXVII (February 1, 1950), 148-
        50.

        A survey of the KKK's status throughout the South,
        what it is doing to increase its membership, and
        what local and state authorities are doing to curb
        its activities.

F491   _____.   "What the Klan Did in Indiana." New Re-
        public, LII (November 16, 1927), 330-32.

        A report on the political activities of Klan leader
        David C. Stephenson in Indiana before his convic-
        tion for murder.

F492   "Then School Bells Rang." Newsweek, LX (September
        17, 1962), 31-32+.

        KKK activities increase as Negroes attempt to in-
        tegrate public schools in Georgia and through the
        South.

F493   Thornbrough, Emma Lou.   "Segregation in Indiana
        During the Klan Era of the 1920's." Mississippi
        Valley Historical Review, XLVII (March, 1961),
        594-618.   (Reprinted in Meier, August, and Elliott
        Rudwick, eds.   The Making of Black America; Es-
        says in Negro Life and History.   Vol. II: The

Black Community in Modern America.   New York: Atheneum, 1969.)

An analysis of the discrimination faced by Negroes in Indiana during the '20s and its relationship to KKK activity in that state.

F494   Thornton, J. Mills, III. "Alabama Politics, J. Thomas Heflin, and the Expulsion Movement of 1929. " Alabama Review, XXI (April, 1968), 83-112.

The KKK tries to retain its influence in Alabama politics, while Democratic leaders repudiate the Klan and expel Klan candidates from the party.

F495   Toll, William. "Progress and Piety: The Ku Klux Klan and Social Change in Tillamook, Oregon. " Pacific Northwest Quarterly, LXIX (April, 1978), 75-85.

A study of the organization and development of the KKK in the Oregon community of Tillamook. An analysis of the socioeconomic backgrounds of Klan members is provided in an effort to determine causes for the existence of the Klan and its anti-Catholic policies in Oregon.

F496   Toy, Eckard V. , Jr. "The Ku Klux Klan in Tillamook, Oregon. " Pacific Northwest Quarterly, LIII (April, 1962), 60-64.

KKK activities in an Oregon community are used to illustrate the Klan appeal in Oregon to keep the state "American. "

F497   Tremblay, William C. "Reporter Joins KKK, Finds Tame Yes Men. " Editor & Publisher, C (May 20, 1967), 15.

A Detroit newspaper correspondent infiltrates the local Klan chapter to find it more concerned about financial matters than burning crosses.

F498   "Trial by Jury. " Newsweek, LXVI (November 1, 1965), 36.

A report on the trial of Klansman Collie Wilkins

for the murder of civil-rights worker Viola Liuzzo.

F499   Trillin, Calvin. "U. S. Journal: Luverne, Ala." New Yorker, XLVI (August 29, 1970), 53-58.

The story of an Alabama businessman boycotted by the Klan for refusing to fire a Negro employee whose son was attending a white school.

F500   "Trouble at Charlie's Place." Newsweek, XXXVI (September 11, 1950), 36.

Local police are found participating in a Klan raid on a Negro night spot in South Carolina.

F501   Truzzi, Marcello. "The 100% American Songbag: Conservative Folksongs in America." Western Folklore, XXVIII (1969), 27-40.

This article contains the lyrics of the Klan-inspired folksong "Klansman's Jubilee Song," sung to the tune of "John Brown's Body."

F502   Tyack, David B. "The Perils of Pluralism: The Background of the Pierce Case." American Historical Review, LXXIV (October, 1968), 74-98.

An in-depth analysis of the situation in Oregon that led to the passage of the Klan-sponsored compulsory school bill and the legal controversy that resulted.

F503   "Un-American Klan." Economist, CCXV (April 3, 1965), 48+.

The House Un-American Activities Committee votes to conduct an investigation of the Klan.

F504   "UNC Students Heckle Klan." Southern Patriot, XXXIII (February, 1975), 7.

National KKK leader David Duke is prevented from speaking by protesting students at the University of North Carolina.

F505   "Uncle Henry on the Klan Komplex." Collier's National Weekly, LXXI (January 27, 1923), 15.

Humorously takes the view that the Klan is suffering from an "inferiority complex. "

F506   "United States Court of Appeals Confirms Conviction of Two KKK Members for the Murder of Negro Army Reserve Officer Lemuel A. Penn near Athens, Georgia. " Race Relations Law Reporter, XII (Summer, 1967), 634-43.

A U. S. Appeals Court upholds the convictions of two Klan members in the murder of a Negro army officer.

F507   "United States Court of Appeals Upholds Conviction of KKK Member Who Bombed the House of a Negro Boy Who Attended a Desegregated School in Duval County, Florida. " Race Relations Law Reporter, XII (Summer, 1967), 621-26.

A U. S. Appeals Court upholds the conviction of a Florida Klansman in the bombing of a Negro home.

F508   "United States District Court Gives Klan Member, Who Bombed House of Negro Boy Attending Desegregated School in Duval County, Seven Years Imprisonment for Violation of the Civil Rights Conspiracy Act and for Obstructing a Court Order for Public School Desegregation. " Race Relations Law Reporter, XI (Spring, 1966), 62-69.

The text of a court decision in Florida involving a Klan member trying to change his guilty plea in the bombing of a Negro home.

F509   "United States District Court Issues a Permanent Injunction Enjoining Klan Members from Interfering with Orders of the Court or the Exercise of Civil Rights by Negro Citizens in Washington Parish, La. " Race Relations Law Reporter, X (Winter, 1965), 1449-67.

The text of an injunction issued by the U. S. District Court in New Orleans against the Klan and other right-wing organizations to keep them from interfering with the civil rights of Negro citizens in Louisiana.

F510   "United States District Court Issues an Injunction Restraining the K. K. K., the Anti-Communist Christian Association and Certain Individual Klansmen from Interfering with the Civil Rights of Negroes in Washington Parish, Louisiana." Race Relations Law Reporter, XI (Spring, 1966), 53-54.

An injunction from the U. S. District Court in New Orleans restrains the Klan and other groups from interfering with the civil rights of Negroes in Louisiana.

F511 "U. S. Supreme Court Voids Conviction of Klan Leader for Criminal Syndicalism Since Law Fails to Distinguish Between Simple Advocacy and Incitement to Imminent Lawless Action." Race Relations Law Survey, I (November, 1969), 147-48.

The Supreme Court overrules an Ohio court's conviction of a Klan member for remarks he made in a TV interview.

F512 "The University of Oklahoma and the Ku Klux Klan." School and Society, XVI (October 7, 1922), 412-13.

A statement is issued by the University of Oklahoma's Board of Regents concerning the use of school facilities for political meetings, aimed at faculty members involved with pro- or anti-Klan forces.

F513 Van Der Veer, Virginia. "Hugo Black and the K. K. K." American Heritage, XIX (April, 1968), 60-64+.

A report on Black's nomination to the Supreme Court and the controversy that arose when his past connection with the KKK was disclosed.

F514 Vander Zanden, James W. "The Klan Revival." American Journal of Sociology, LXV (March, 1960), 456-62.

An analysis of the people who joined the KKK after the 1954 Brown decision and their positions within the social structure. This study shows that Klan membership is basically comprised of the lower middle class and those concerned with symbols of social status.

F515   "The Various Shady Lives of the Ku Klux Klan. "
        Time, LXXXV (April 9, 1965), 24-25.

        (See C50.)

F516   Verlie, Lester.   "The Klan Rides the South Again. "
        Collier's National Weekly, CXXII (October 9, 1948),
        13-15+.

        The KKK finds new strength in the South as the
        civil-rights issue begins to take shape.

F517   "Vile Bodies. "   Economist, CCLXIV (July 9, 1977),
        36.

        A brief overview of recent incidents involving the
        KKK, including the fight between black Marines and
        Klan members at Camp Pendleton and the Klan rally
        near Plains, Georgia, into which a man drove his
        car.

F518   "Violence and the KKK. "   Nation, CC (April 19, 1965),
        406-7.

        Martin Luther King, Jr. , of the Southern Christian
        Leadership Conference states his opposition to the
        House Un-American Activities Committee's investi-
        gation of the Ku Klux Klan.

F519   "Violence Comes to a Southern Town. "   Ebony, XXX
        (December, 1974), 148-50+.

        A report on the making of a film from William B.
        Huie's The Klansman (see E84), a novel about the
        modern-day KKK in Alabama.

F520   "The Violence Trap. "   Nation, CCX (March 8, 1970),
        261.

        A report of an FBI attempt to apprehend Klansmen
        involved with some bombings in Mississippi, which
        resulted in the death of a female Klan member.

F521   Wakefield, Dan.   "Eye of the Storm. "   Nation, CXC
        (May 7, 1960), 396-405.

        A report on conditions in Montgomery, Alabama, in

the years after the bus boycott finds the KKK still active in this southern city.

F522   Ware, Edward T., A Texan, and Edward T. Devine. "The Ku Klux Klan." Survey, XLVIII (May 14, 1922), 251-53.

Three letters to the editor: the ones by Ware and "a Texan" criticize Devine's earlier articles (see F115 and F116) for his lack of condemnation of the Klan; in the third letter, Devine tries to defend his original statements.

F523   Warwick, Loy. "Father's Private Miracle." Coronet, XLIV (August, 1958), 19-23.

The story of a backwoods preacher and how he broke up a KKK meeting by himself.

F524   "WBOX and the KKK." Newsweek, LXVI (August 16, 1965), 75.

A Louisiana radio station challenges the Klan by encouraging the avoidance of racial conflict.

F525   Wesberry, James P. "K. K. K. Holds Cross-Burning Near Atlanta." Christian Century, LXXIV (January 9, 1957), 54.

A news report of a big Klan rally held outside Atlanta.

F526   Wesley, Al. "Klan on Upsurge in Urban U. S." Guardian, XXVII (January 22, 1975), 7.

A report on an increase of KKK membership and activity in some northern cities.

F527   "What Is Wrong with the Klan?" Nation, CXVIII (June 18, 1924), 698.

Editorial comment that the spirit of intolerance, which the KKK represents, is more threatening than the Klan itself.

F528   "What the 'Sit-ins' Are Stirring Up." U. S. News & World Report, XLVIII (April 18, 1960), 52-54+.

A survey of increasing Klan activity in the South as a response to the developing civil-rights movement.

F529 "When Carolina Indians Went on the Warpath. " U. S. News & World Report, XLIV (January 31, 1958), 14.

A report of a KKK rally in North Carolina broken up by a group of local Indians.

F530 White, Arthur C. "An American Fascismo. " Forum, LXXII (November, 1924), 636-42.

An analogy is drawn between the Klan and what it wants for America and the deeds of the Fascist regime in Italy.

F531 White, Walter F. "Election by Terror in Florida. " New Republic, XXV (January 12, 1921), 195-97.

A report of Klan activities in Florida aimed at preventing Negroes from voting in the 1920 election.

F532 _____. "Reviving the Ku Klux Klan. " Forum, LXV (April, 1921), 426-34.

A report of the "revival" and growth of the KKK and the reception it has been receiving.

F533 White, William A. "Annihilate the Klan!" Nation, CXX (January 7, 1925), 7.

A statement of the harm the KKK has brought to America, especially its negative effect on liberal ideals.

F534 _____. "Patience and Publicity. " World Tomorrow, VII (March, 1924), 87.

The position is taken that the best way to counter the intolerance of the KKK is to remain patient against Klan attacks and try to expose the lies and activities of the KKK in the press.

F535 White, William L. "A Voice from Main Street, U. S. A. " Survey Graphic, XXVIII (February, 1939), 133-35.

The Klan's belief in democracy, nonmilitary uniforms, and use of committees to control the organization are seen as positive elements when compared with the Nazi/Fascist movements in Europe.

F536 Whitehead, Don. "Murder in Mississippi: Attack on Terror." Reader's Digest, XCVII (September, 1970), 191-96+.

An excerpt from the author's work on the Klan's murder of three civil-rights workers in Mississippi (see E188).

F537 "Why Kansas Bans the Klan." Literary Digest, LXXV (November 11, 1922), 13.

A report on the decision of the governor of Kansas to try to expel the Klan from that state in response to recent activities of the KKK.

F538 "Why They Join the Klan." New Republic, XXXVI (November 21, 1923), 321-22.

A brief analysis of the KKK and its appeal in various sections of the country in the wake of increasing Klan membership.

F539 Wieck, Agnes. "Ku Kluxing in the Miners' Country." New Republic, XXXVIII (March 26, 1924), 122-24.

A report of confrontations between Klan members and Catholic immigrants in the coal-mining region of southern Illinois.

F540 "William Allen White's War on the Klan." Literary Digest, LXXXIII (October 11, 1924), 16.

A Kansas newspaper editor runs for governor on an anti-Klan platform.

F541 Williams, Dennis A., Lea Donosky, and Martin Kasindorf. "The Great White Hope." Newsweek, XC (November 14, 1977), 45.

A profile on Klan leader David Duke and his attempts to draw middle-class, "respectable" whites into the KKK.

F542 Williams, Dennis A. , Eleanor Clift, and William Schmidt. "The Klan Also Rises. " Newsweek, LXXXVII (January 12, 1976), 33-34.

A report on the attempts of the KKK to appeal to the middle-class white population and increase the prestige and influence of the Klan.

F543 Williams, Dennis A. , and William J. Cook. "Mistaken Identity. " Newsweek, LXXXVIII (December 13, 1976), 35+.

Black Marines attack a Klan meeting being held on base at Camp Pendleton, California.

F544 Williams, Donald E. "Protest Under the Cross: The Ku Klux Klan Presents Its Case to the Public, 1960. " Southern Speech Journal, XXVII (1961), 43-55.

A survey of the reaction to renewed Klan activity in the wake of the Supreme Court's school-desegregation decision.

F545 Wilson, William E. "That Long, Hot Summer in Indiana. " American Heritage, XVI (August, 1965), 56-64.

Reminiscences of the summer of 1924, when the author's father, a U. S. Representative, was campaigning for re-election against the Klan.

F546 "With Malice Aforethought. " Time, LV (March 13, 1950), 24.

Klansmen are arrested in Alabama after one of their "raids" leaves a man dead, while another KKK member commits suicide.

F547 "W. L. Davis, Imperial Wizard of the Ku Klux Klan, Inciting a Gathering. " Illustrated London News, CCXXXVIII (January 21, 1961), 94.

A photo of the Imperial Wizard addressing a Klan rally in Florida.

F548 Wolf, Horace J. , George E. Haynes, and John Keresey.

"How Shall We Meet the Klan?" World Tomorrow, VII (March, 1924), 85-86.

The authors present their views on how Negroes, Catholics, and Jews should respond to attacks by the Ku Klux Klan.

F549 Wooten, James R. "Cross Burning in Florida--1975 Style. " U. S. News & World Report, LXXVIII (June 23, 1975), 34.

A KKK rally and cross-burning in Florida is open to the public as the Klan tries to bolster its public image.

F550 Wrench, Evelyn. "English-Speaking World. " Spectator, CXXX (March 24, 1923), 506-07.

A brief report on the outcome of the murder trial of a number of Klan members in Mer Rouge, Louisiana, and a report on KKK attempts to organize in Canada.

F551 "Wrapt in Mystery. " Nation and Athenaeum, XXXII (January 6, 1923), 544-45.

A brief article describing the organization and activities of the KKK.

F552 Young, Pete. "A Few Soft Words for the Ku Klux Klan. " Esquire, LXXII (July, 1969), 104-05+.

A report of a visit with Grand Dragon J. R. Jones of the North Carolina Klan before he started a one-year jail sentence for contempt of Congress. Jones talked about recent Klan activity in North Carolina.

F553 _____. "Rainbow Sign. " Katallagete, III (Fall, 1971), 31-37.

F554 Zilg, Jerry. "Militant Youth, Labor Confront KKK Rally. " Worker's World, XIII (June 25, 1971), 2.

A KKK rally in Maryland leads to a confrontation between Klansmen and left-wing students and workers.

ALABAMA   A1, A70, B4, B31, B48, B89, B90, B116, C38,
   C40, C47, C53, D24, E6, E21, E38, E79, E84, E139,
   E140, F6, F7, F35, F41, F72, F134, F146, F149, F151,
   F198, F222, F242, F296, F363, F377, F445, F450, F451,
   F456, F469, F490, F494, F498, F519, F546
   Birmingham   E50, F57, F287
   Crenshaw County   F478
   Huntsville   A18
   Mobile   F150, F483
   Montgomery   F521
   Tuskegee   F439

ALLEN, HENRY   F92, F233, F462

AMERICAN LEGION   F445

AMERICAN NAZI PARTY   E27, E150

AMES, ADLEBERT   B97

ANTI-ALIENISM   E37, E53, E54, E59, E65, E80, E145,
   E162, E185, F120, F134, F152, F231, F404, F465

ANTI-CATHOLICISM   D4, E8, E37, E51, E53, E59, E65,
   E80, E90, E103, E104, E132, E141, E142, E144, E145,
   E155, E185, E186, E187, E191, F67, F75, F99, F104,
   F120, F134, F139, F152, F195, F231, F328, F354, F375,
   F378, F421, F440, F461, F465, F495

ANTI-KLAN ACTIVITIES   A8, A57, A77, B2, B27, B28,
   B48, B81, B82, C5, E106, F21, F33, F84, F122, F137,
   F153, F238, F258, F261, F334, F364, F438

ANTI-KLAN LEGISLATION   (See also Ku Klux Klan Act)
   A5, B10, B13, B19, B21, B28, B29, B30, B37, B44,
   B49, B56, B66, B69, B79, B92, C5, C7, D102, E10,

EVANS, HIRAM W.   D13,   E1,   E12,   E19,   E24,   E31,   E52,
    E53,   E54,   E55,   E64,   E88,   E93,   E104,   E119,   E131,
    E162,   E176,   E177,   E191,   F9,   F10,   F14,   F34,   F36,   F81,
    F90,   F128,   F134,   F138,   F139,   F140,   F141,   F163,   F166,
    F251,   F268,   F278,   F286,   F288,   F337,   F359,   F361,   F406,
    F449,   F469

FASCISM   F278,   F443,   F530,   F535

FEDERAL BUREAU OF INVESTIGATION (FBI)   E85,   E120,
    E124,   E188,   F33,   F85,   F86,   F96,   F148,   F153,   F203,
    F241,   F272,   F346,   F369,   F475,   F477,   F520,   F536

FERGUSON, JAMES   E1,   F341

FERGUSON, MIRIAM "MA"   E1,   E20,   F10,   F341

FLORIDA   A4,   B33,   D40,   D72,   E26,   E100,   E140,   F78,
    F248,   F267,   F313,   F490,   F531,   F547,   F549
    Duval County   F507,   F508
    Miami   F410
    St. Augustine   E184,   F315,   F344
    Tampa   E159

FLOWERS, RICHMOND   F149,   F289

FORREST, NATHAN B.   A78,   B17,   B29,   B63,   B118,   E93

FREEDMAN'S BUREAU   B64,   C36

FREEDOM RIDES   E21,   E123

FUQUA, HENRY   F39

GARVEY, MARCUS   E33,   E41,   E48,   E57

GEORGIA   A22,   A24,   A30,   A45,   A75,   B10,   B25,   B29,   B87,
    B89,   B102,   B109,   C39,   D13,   D34,   D48,   D54,   D58,   D72,
    E15,   E26,   E38,   E94,   E140,   F23,   F24,   F52,   F55,   F82,
    F119,   F136,   F151,   F155,   F201,   F206,   F216,   F309,   F310,
    F345,   F366,   F367,   F372,   F373,   F385,   F413,   F415,   F416,
    F434,   F442,   F444,   F490,   F492,   F506
    Atlanta   E89,   F421,   F525
    Columbus   F446
    Pine Mountain   F389
    Plains   F517
    Stone Mountain   F4,   F324,   F343

LEA, JOHN W.   C27

LINDSEY, BEN B.   F334, F335

LITTLEFIELD, MILTON S.   B33

LIUZZO, MRS. VIOLA   E6, E123, E128, F369, F377, F498

LOCKE, JOHN G.   F347

LOUISIANA   A17, A38, B47, B89, C12, D1, D31, D88, E2,
    E140, F39, F63, F76, F77, F151, F209, F321, F424,
    F479
    Bogalusa   F173, F524
    Lafayette Parish   A20
    Mer Rouge   D10, D83, E44, E49, E148, F83, F123,
    F126, F302, F359, F374, F550
    New Orleans   B77, F473
    Shreveport   D55
    Washington Parish   F509, F510

LOYLESS, THOMAS   F446

LUMBEE INDIANS   F28, F42, F97, F193, F212, F214,
    F215, F380, F529

McADOO, WILLIAM G.   E96, F16, F62

MADDOX, LESTER   E15

MAINE   F88

MARSHALL, LOUIS   E149

MARYLAND   B30, F554
    Baltimore   F31

MASSACHUSETTS
    Boston   E137, F340, F352, F481, F526

MICHIGAN   D16, D70, E26, F290
    Detroit   E89, F476, F497
    Pontiac   F131, F190

MILITIA, NEGRO   A3, B3, B68, B91, B100, B117

MINNESOTA   D51, F333
    Minneapolis   F188